Handbags

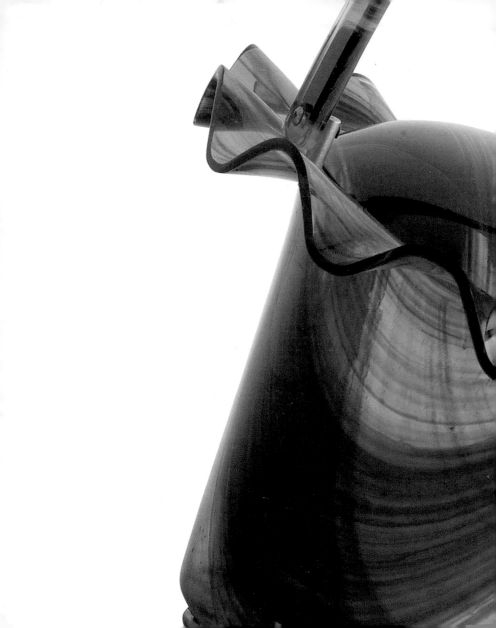

Handbags

JUDITH MILLER

LONDON, NEW YORK,
MUNICH, MELBOURNE, DELHI

A joint production from DK and THE PRICE GUIDE COMPANY

DORLING KINDERSLEY LIMITED
Editor Katie John
Designers Lee Riches, Katie Eke
DTP, Reproduction, and Design Adam Walker
Production Elizabeth Warman
Managing Art Editor Heather McCarry

THE PRICE GUIDE COMPANY LIMITED
Publishing Manager Julie Brooke   **Editor** Jessica Bishop
Editorial Assistants Dan Dunlavey and Sandra Lange
Digital Image Co-ordinator Ellen Sinclair
Photographer Graham Rae

While every care has been taken in the compilation of this guide, neither the authors nor the publishers accept any liability for any financial or other loss incurred by reliance placed on the information contained in *Handbags*.

First published in the USA in 2006 by DK Publishing, Inc.
375 Hudson Street, New York, NY 10014

First published in Great Britain in 2006 by Dorling Kindersley Limited,
80 Strand, London WC2R 0RL
A Penguin Company

The Price Guide Company (UK) Ltd: info@thepriceguidecompany.com

2 4 6 8 10 9 7 5 3 1

CIP catalog records for this book are available from the Library of Congress and the British Library.

UK ISBN-13: 978 1 4053 0626 3
UK ISBN-10: 1 4053 0626 2

US ISBN-13: 978-0-7566-1920-6
US ISBN-10: 0-7566-1920-3

Proofing by Colourscan, Singapore
Printed in China by Hung Hing Offset Printing Company Ltd

Discover more at
www.dk.com

CONTENTS

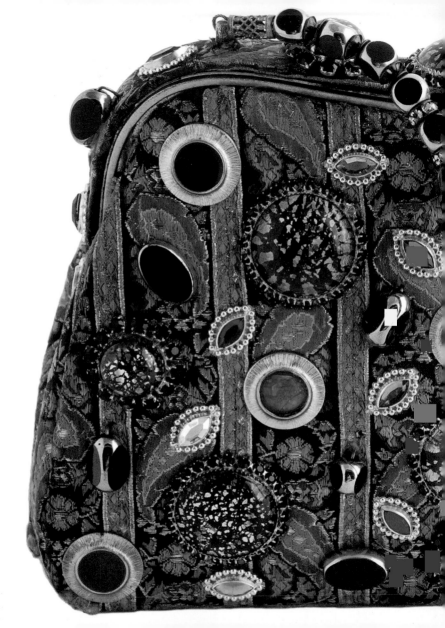

INTRODUCTION

A survey has found that an American woman owns an average of six handbags. A quick telephone call to my friends on both sides of the Atlantic suggests that these women are the exception rather than the norm – and that one of my friends owns so many bags she can't possibly hope to use them all, even if she used a different bag every day for six months.

   Whether you believe, like Miss Piggy, that "it is vital to have at least one handbag for each ... social occasion" or that, like my friend, you can never have too many bags, I'm sure you will find this collection an inspiration.

Judith Miller.

Star Ratings

Each of the handbags in this book has a star rating according to its value:

★ $50–200; £25–100 ★★ $200–500; £100–250 ★★★ $500–1,000; £250–500

★★★★ $1,000–2,000; £500–1,000 ★★★★★ $2,000 upward; £1,000 upward

PRE-1890

The modern handbag is the descendent of a number of historical bags: the Medieval girdle pouch and almoner, the 18th-century pocket, purse, and work bag, the 19th-century reticule and chatelaine. Like today's clutch bags, totes, and rucksacks, these ancient bags were designed to carry money and other valuables, sewing materials, books, cosmetics, visiting cards, and pens. Many bags were decorated with exquisite embroidery or beading.

While few examples of these early bags exist outside museums today, they provide a fascinating insight into the evolution of the handbag and an inspiration to handbag designers now and in the future.

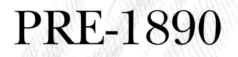

Turkish bag made for the European market: red velvet with gold embroidery and drawstring closure.   *19th century*   ★★☆☆☆

EMBROIDERED

Petit-point bag with pink roses on a brown ground, gilt metal
frame, and chain handle.   *19th century*   ★★ ☆☆☆

Silk drawstring bag with embroidered decoration; lined with satin. *Late 18th century* ★★★☆☆

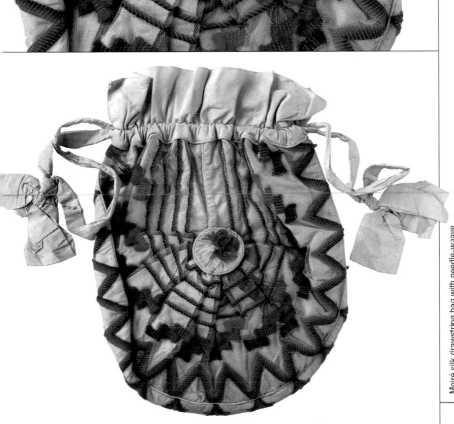

Moiré silk drawstring bag with needle-weave
decoration. *c.1820* ★ ★ ☆ ☆ ☆

★★★★★

Rare Pennsylvania silk and linen sampler purse, stitched by "M. Morto₁," with floral spray design and polychrome alphabet. *Late 18th century*

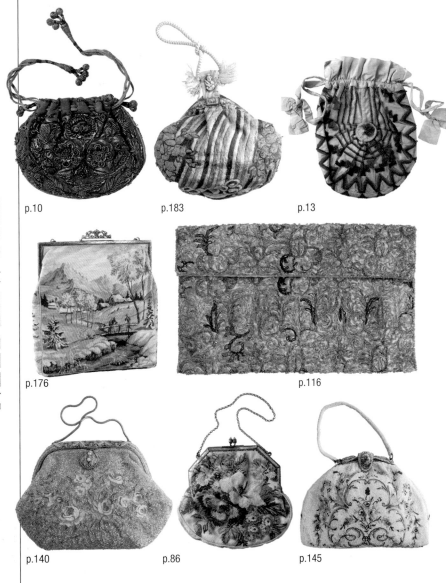

NEEDLEWORK

p.10

p.183

p.13

p.176

p.116

p.140

p.86

p.145

p.85

p.19

p.80

p.155

p.330

p.152

p.44

p.14

NEEDLEWORK

Georgian card purse with metallic
embroidery. *1770-1780* ★ ★ ★ ☆ ☆

EMBROIDERED

English silk purse, embroidered on both sides with crewelwork, metallic braid, and sequins. This side shows Archangel Michael. *Late 17th–early 18th century* ★★★★★

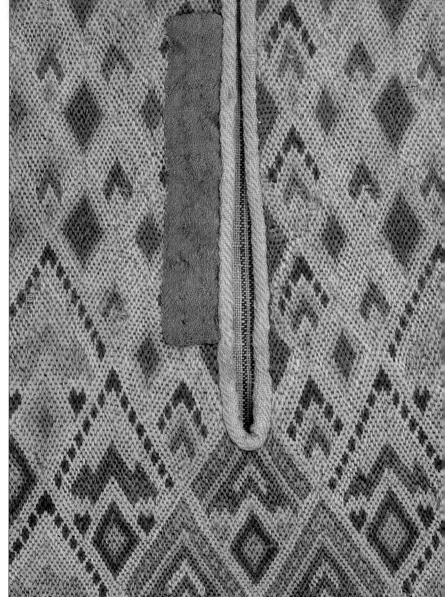

DETAIL: Design on pocket.

POCKETS

During the 17th century, dresses had full skirts; this made it possible for women to carry items such as smelling salts, mirrors, fans, and even small liquor bottles in their clothes without ruining the silhouette. To do so they used flat pockets, usually pear-shaped or oval with squared corners, which were tied beneath the skirt at each hip and could be accessed by slits in the skirt fabric.

It was not until the 1790s that fashions changed radically and bulky pockets became impractical. The popular new "Empire" dress was too sleek to conceal belongings; however, women were reluctant to give up the convenience of having their precious things readily to hand. The solution was to take pockets out from under the skirt and carry them by hand. Thus the modern handbag was born.

Florentine work stick pocket, probably from Chester County, PA. Executed in shades of red, blue, and yellow, and initialed "SI;" repaired.   *1761*   ★★★★

FIGURAL BAGS

Figures and animals have been favorite motifs since the 18th century, when bags first became major fashion accessories. As the production of samplers and other pretty fabric items became a popular leisure pastime, carefully worked figural scenes began to appear on ornate needlework bags. Beadwork bags were also adorned with complex figures and animals; these bags, rather than bags with floral or abstract bead designs, are the ones that most attract collectors' attention today.

From 1910 to 1930 designs were inspired by flowers, chinoiserie (oriental motifs), eastern carpets, romantic medieval castles, and Venetian scenes. The images were often taken from popular prints or famous tapestries.

Exported from France, Germany, and Italy, these bags were time-consuming to make and import, and therefore costly when new. They still command higher prices today, especially if they have survived in good condition.

"While men wear their hands in their pockets so grand,
The ladies have pockets to wear in their hand."
THE IMPERIAL WEEKLY GAZETTE, 1804

Beaded drawstring bag with figural
lakeside scene and floral border.
19th century ★ ☆ ☆ ☆

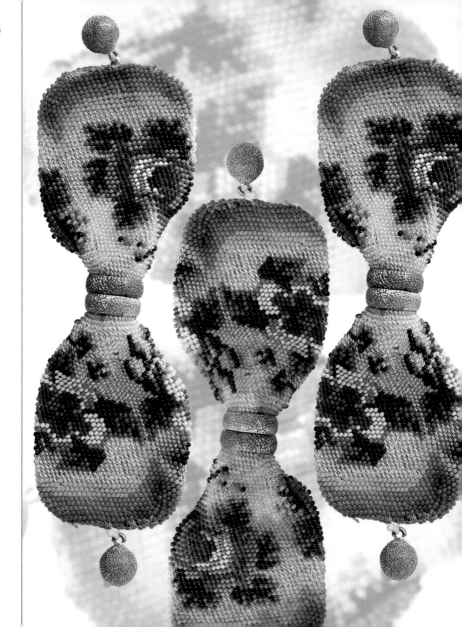

MISER'S PURSE

An early take on the unisex bag, the miser's purse first became popular in the late 18th century. Also called a stocking, ring, or long purse, this bag was designed to hold coins. The bag gained its name because it was difficult for people to take money from it.

The miser's purse was generally long and flat in shape and was sealed around the edges. The middle section, which was left undecorated, had a slit for access; it was gathered by sliding rings, thus forming distinct pouches at each end. Sliding the rings closed would securely store the coins in the pouches. In some bags, the two ends were differently shaped, and were probably intended to store two different types of coin. Bags were often made from crocheted or knitted silk thread and decorated with cut-steel beads.

By the late 19th century, miser's purses had largely been replaced by leather purses; however, patterns for making them appeared in women's magazines right up to the early 20th century.

A beaded miser's purse with roses decoration and ormolu rings and balls. ★ ☆☆☆☆

Beaded sewing purse with floral design.
Early 18th century ★★★☆☆

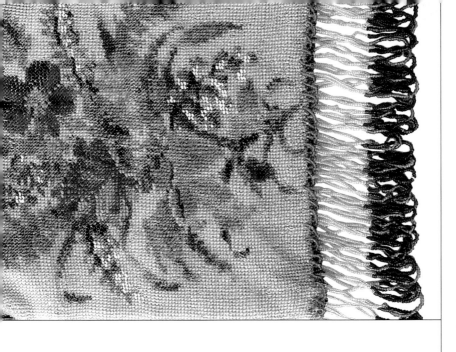

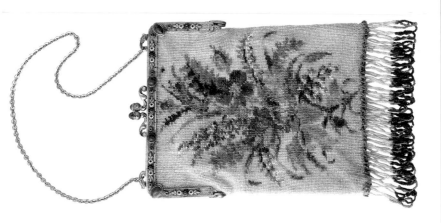

Beaded purse, possibly French, decorated with a spray of flowers on a white ground; also has fringe, gilt metal jeweled clasp, and chain handle. *1870s* ★ ☆☆☆

Beadwork purse, hand-worked on black velvet with flowers
and the name "Emily M Hollister." *c.1810*   ★★★★☆

HOME-MADE BAGS

The ability to sew has historically been seen as an important accomplishment for refined young women and an essential skill for less wealthy ones. Frames and handles for bags could be bought separately for the creative-minded to embellish at home. Each bag could be designed to complement a favorite outfit and would be unique. Home-made needlework bags are perhaps the easiest to come by; figural and landscape scenes tend to catch collectors' eyes, especially if the delicate material shows little sign of damage or wear.

In the 20th century, a growth in leisure time, and the high price of one-off designer accessories, ensured that people continued to make their own bags. During the Second World War, women created bags from fabric scraps, beads, and costume jewelry. In the 1960s and 1970s, the fashion for hippy crafts led women to decorate shop-bought bags with needlework, stickers, or découpage. The craze for customization shows no sign of dying out today.

INSET: The reverse side of the purse.

PRE-1890

STRAW BASKETS

The technique for weaving baskets from natural materials, such as straw, wood, and leaves, has been practiced around the world for thousands of years. The oldest woven baskets still in existence originate from Egypt and are thought to be over 10,000 years old.

During the 19th century, makers in the US produced a wide variety of woven baskets. Various shapes were developed, for practical uses such as collecting eggs or carrying flowers. Toward the end of the century, baskets started to be made as tourist souvenirs. These included Nantucket baskets, which have become one of this island's signature products. The baskets are based on the shape of a traditional barrel and may be embellished with scrimshaw plaques. They are still made by Nantucket craftsmen today.

Baskets made elsewhere in the US could be decorated with a painted design or woven with alternating bands of colored straw.

Painted and finely woven reeded basket purse with two swing handles, from Lancaster County, PA.   *19th century*   ★ ☆ ☆ ☆

1890s–1920s

As women started to become independent, they needed handbags to suit many occasions – a generous leather bag for traveling, a tiny purse for shopping trips, a beaded or embroidered bag for evenings.

During the 1920s, early plastics started to be used to make handbag bodies and frames, although leather and fabric bags made with metal – even solid silver – frames continued to be popular.

By the end of the period, the Jazz Age had taken hold, and Flapper girls were dancing the Charleston with delicate beaded purses hanging from their wrists.

Pale blue beadwork réticule, with cream cotton lining and navy blue silk top and drawstring.   *c.1900*   ★ ☆☆☆☆

Beadwork bag with beaded fringe.
Late 19th century ★ ☆☆☆☆

Beadwork bag with repeating blue and gold design, tassel, and drawstring closure. *c.1890* ★☆☆☆☆

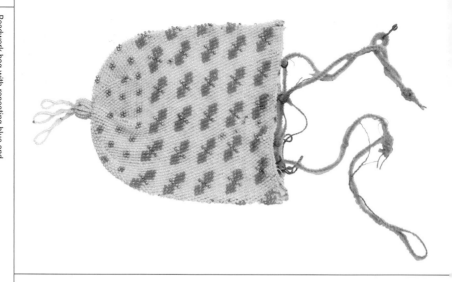

Beadwork bag with floral decoration and tassel, gilt metal frame, and chain strap. *c.1900* ★★☆☆☆

"Fashion is made to become unfashionable."
COCO CHANEL

☆☆☆
★★★

"Puffy" beaded purse, with pale blue geometric
design on b'own ground, gold-tone clasp, beaded
handle, and blue silk lining.

DETAIL: Close-up of moth decoration.

BEADING

Beaded bags are the most collectable and often the most valuable vintage bags – a reflection of the hours of work that went into them, and of their fragile nature. The bright colors and intricate workmanship often make them more suited to display than to use, but that does not diminish their appeal.

Beaded bags have been popular since the early 19th century. In the 1910s and 1920s, manufacturers used Venetian or Bohemian beads. Venetian beads are very small, slightly iridescent, and with a pure color that does not fade. Bohemian beads tend to be larger and coarser and to fade over time. Clasps and handles are usually metal and often inset with glass or semi-precious stones. Bags were often lined with silk, which may have deteriorated far more than the exterior. A sympathetic replacement can enhance the value of a bag.

When buying beaded bags, consider whether the design suits the beads from which it is made.

Art Nouveau beaded purse with moth design, and with jeweled gilt metal clasp and chain strap. ★★★★★

Richly detailed Art Nouveau beaded bag, with celluloid clasp. *c.1900* ★★★ ★★☆

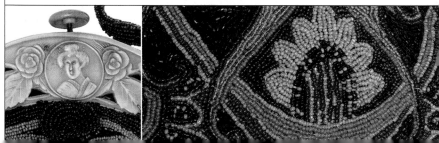

Purse with unusual decoration including trapunto, chain stitch, and beadlike French knots; also has rose gold effect frame and chain strap.

★★★ ☆☆

Metallic and satin réticule, lined with
red cotton. *1900s* ★☆☆☆☆

Beaded purse with jet-black ground and multi-colored geometric motif; also has very early plastic clasp and chain-link handle. ★★★☆

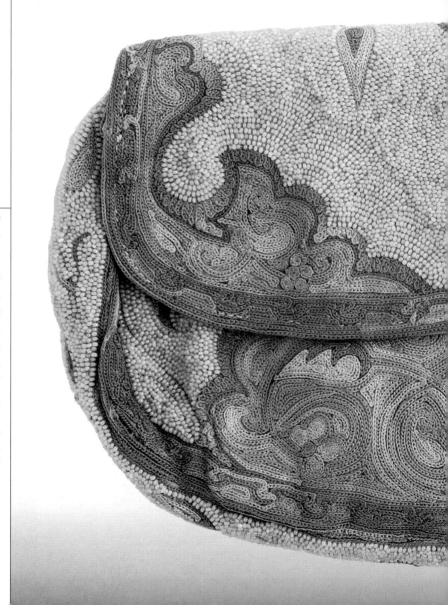

French purse with embroidered paisley design and cream beads. Cream silk interior has gilt stamp, "xxx de vie Paris France," pocket, and handheld mirror. *Early 20th century* ★★☆☆☆

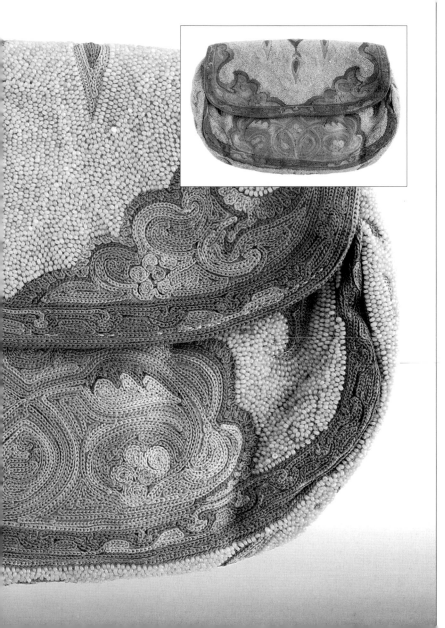

Micro-beaded purse with floral decoration, intricate fringe, heavy silver frame, and silver chain strap. ★★★★☆

Floral beaded bag, the elaborate gilt metal
clasp set with faux rubies, moonstones, and
turquoise.   *Early 20th century*   ★ ☆☆☆☆

BEADED BEAUTY

p.48

p.54

p.76

p.150

p.164

p.154

p.46

p.71

p.75

p.77

p.129

p.126

p.316

p.124

p.42

BEADED BEAUTY

Silver beadwork réticule with pink cotton ground and beaded tassel and handle. *c.1910* ★☆☆☆☆

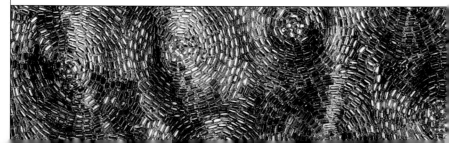

Beadwork réticule with bird design, black silk lining, and looped fringe. *c.1910* ★ ☆☆☆☆

German beaded purse, decorated on both sides; also has ornate fringe, embossed silver frame, silver chain strap, and leather interior. ★★★ ★★☆ ☆☆

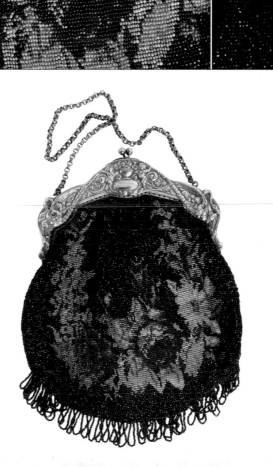

Beaded purse with colored flower garlands on black
iridescent ground, black looped fringe, and sterling
silver frame and chain. ★★★★☆
★★★★

Silk clutch bag with antique-gold ground and oriental-style decoration. Also has gilt metal filigree frame and clasp set with faux jade.   *c.1915*   ★★★☆☆

Large beaded handbag with roses on beige ground; also has fringes, silver-plated clasp, and chain strap. ★ ★ ★ ☆ ☆

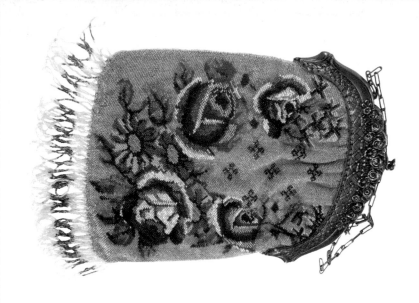

Gray crochet and steel beadwork réticule with chain drawstring. *1910s* ★ ☆ ☆ ☆ ☆

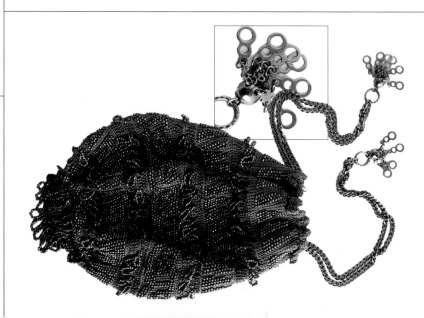

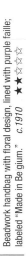

Beadwork handbag with floral design, lined with purple faille; labeled "Made in Be gium."   *c.1910*   ★ ★ ☆ ☆ ☆

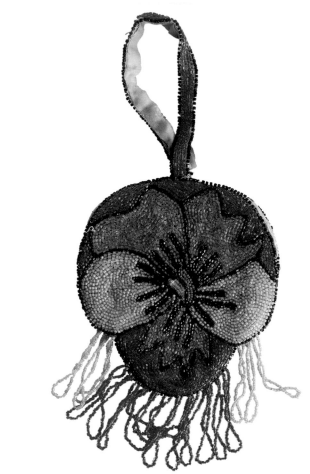

Beadwork "pansy" handbag, with cream silk lining labeled "Hand Made in Belgium." *c.1915* ★★☆☆☆

Small, unlined beadwork handbag.
Early 20th century ★ ☆☆☆☆

Green glass beadwork purse with cylindrical body, tucked "loose" covering, and brown silk lining. Lid has mirror inside. *1920s* ★☆☆☆☆

Gold silk purse with rows of clear yellow beads, columns of
orange rhinestones, gilt metal frame, and chain strap; lined
with cream silk.　*1920s*　★ ☆ ☆ ☆ ☆

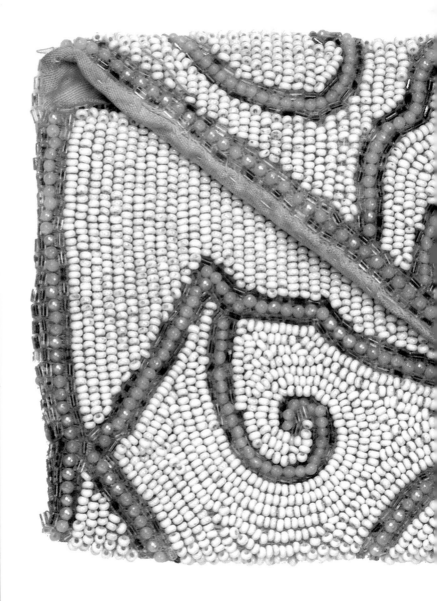

Art Deco cream beaded evening bag. *c.*1920 ★☆☆☆

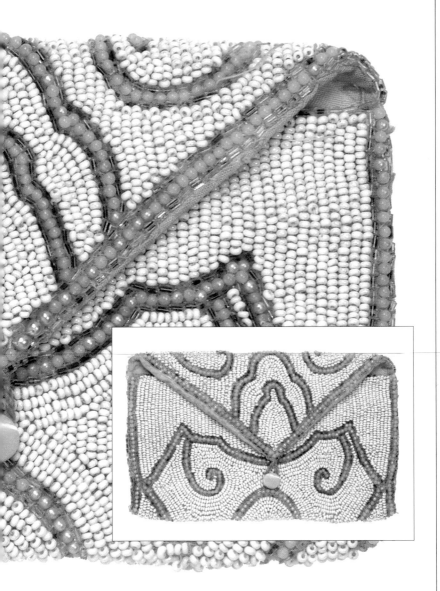

Crocheted handbag with iridescent beads; also has white metal frame and chain strap. *1910–1920* ★★☆☆☆

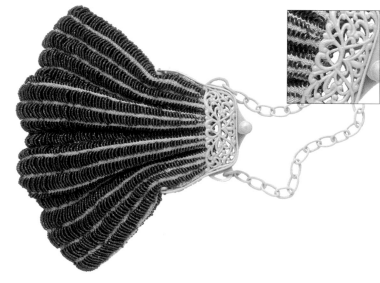

Handbag with iridescent blue beads, filigree celluloid frame, and chain-link strap. *1920s* ★★☆☆☆

Handbag with black glass and cut steel beads, white metal clasp, and chain handle. ★★☆☆☆

Beaded handbag with multi-colored organic design and triangular fringe; also has faux-tortoiseshell Lucite clasp and Lucite chain strap. *1920s* ★★★☆☆

Beaded evening bag with floral design, beaded fringe, gilt metal frame with bead-decorated clasp, and chain strap. *1920s* ★★☆☆☆

French evening bag with micro-beading, beaded fringe, and gilt clasp and chain strap. *1920s* ★★★☆☆

Gold and silver lamé bag with floral decoration, gilt clasp, and chain strap. *1920s* ★☆☆☆☆

Art Deco bag with abstract design in metallic beads, beaded fringe, and gilt metal frame and chain strap. ★ ★ ☆ ☆ ☆

Evening bag with floral beaded design and beaded fringe. Also has gilt metal frame set with semiprecious stones; clasp with colored rhinestone; and chain strap.   *1920s*   ★★☆☆☆

*The bag still has the original fabric
lining, in excellent condition.*

Beaded bag with abstract ethnic design, black and white beaded fringe, and tortoiseshell-effect Lucite clasp and strap.   *1920s*   ★★☆☆☆

Art Deco beadwork bag with floral design on blue ground and faux tortoiseshell celluloid frame. *c.1925* ★ ☆☆☆☆

Art Deco beadwork bag with stylized design on pink ground, looped frirnge, and gilt metal frame and chain strap. *c.1925* ★★ ☆☆

ART DECO STYLE

p.111

p.182

p.202

p.100

p.73

p.112

p.102

p.97

p.131

p.98

p.192

p.136

p.69

p.167

p.211

p.191

ART DECO STYLE

North American Indian purse with embroidered design; made for export. *c.1900* ★★☆☆☆

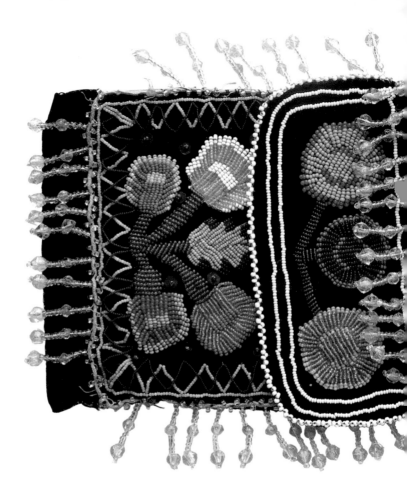

Native American beaded bag with loop handle.
Late 19th–early 20th century ★★☆☆☆

Iroquois beaded box purse, in good condition. These bags were made for the tourist market. *c.1905* ★★☆☆☆

North American Indian felt purse with embroidery
and beaded fringe.   *19th century*   ★ ☆ ☆
★ ★ ☆

Petit-point needlework bag, with floral design. The white metal clasp is set with pearlized panels. *c.1900*

★★★
★☆☆

☆☆☆
★★

Brocade bag with white metal clasp and chain handle. *1920s*

Tapestry purse with gilt metal frame and chain strap, and cream silk lining. *1920s* ★★☆☆☆

The design features an 18th-century Watteau-style pastoral scene in a border of scrolling motifs and flowers.

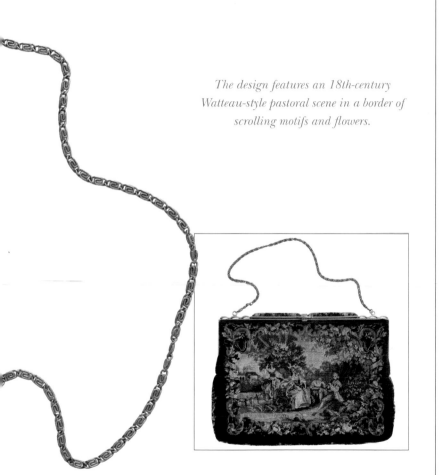

American pouch-style linen handbag, with embroidered blue peacock design and drawstring top.   *1910s*   ★☆☆☆☆

Tapestry petit-point bag with design of rural scene. *1920s* ☆☆☆ ★★

Floral tapestry purse. Gilt metal frame has enameled metal scrolling
motifs and glass cabochons. Interior has cream silk lining and
suede-covered hand mirror. *c.1910* ★ ☆☆☆☆

EMBROIDERED

Austrian petit-point bag, with ormolu and marcasite frame. *1920s* ★ ☆☆☆☆

French cut steel handbag with fringe, and with gilt metal clasp and handles. *c.1910* ★★☆☆☆

"Luxury is a necessity that begins where necessity ends."

COCO CHANEL

French-cut steel handbag with floral motif; also has gilt metal clasp and chain straps. *c.1910*   ★★☆☆☆

DETAIL: Interior of bag, with gold lining and coordinating purse.

METAL MESH BAGS

It was in the 1820s that handbags were first made from precious metals. By the end of the 19th century, mesh coin and finger purses, inspired by the trend for Medieval fashion, were in vogue; however, they were hand-made and therefore expensive. In 1908, A.C. Pratt of Newark, New Jersey patented a mesh machine, enabling people to make affordable, mass-produced bags and, by 1912, mesh bags were all the rage.

The major manufacturers included Whiting and Davis, probably the biggest and most famous mesh bag maker and still making mesh bags today, and the Mandalian Manufacturing Co. of North Attleboro, Massachusets, which closed in the 1940s.

In the 1920s it became possible to screen-print designs onto the mesh. As a result, bags could be made in a rainbow of colors and designs, including enamel and pearlized finishes.

Art Deco evening bag with gold and silver cut-steel beads, Spanish fringe, and gold-tone chain strap. ★ ☆☆☆☆

French Art Deco "Flapper" handbag: mesh purse with rhinestones, brass frame, and decorative tassel.   *c.1925*   ★★★☆☆

Enameled mesh handbag, with metal clasp in Art
Nouveau design. *c.1920* ★ ☆☆☆☆

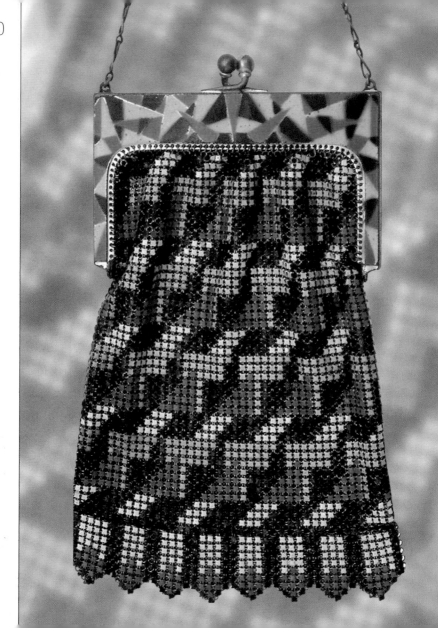

WHITING & DAVIS

The Whiting & Davis company has become synonymous with high-quality mesh bags. These have been produced from the company's inception in 1876, in Plainville, Massachusetts, to the 1940s and beyond.

Prior to 1910, the mesh was made by hand using soldered silver loops, but the process was mechanized by 1920. Early bags tended to be fairly plain, although some top-of-the range examples featured ornate jeweled handles or even tiny clocks. As the 1920s progressed, hues got brighter and patterns became bolder and more geometric. Cheaper ranges sometimes featured printed designs rather than the more typical decoration of colored metals. Some of the most glamorous bags were designed in the 1930s by well-known couturiers such as Elsa Schiaparelli and Paul Poiret.

Mesh bags fell out of favor during the mid-20th century, and Whiting & Davis began to concentrate on other mesh products such as jewelry. However, the bags became popular again during the disco craze of the 1970s.

Whiting & Davis Art Deco mesh purse with enamel geometric decoration on bag and clasp; signed. *1920s* ★ ★ ★ ☆ ☆

Gold lamé bag, with gilt metal clasp set with paste stones. *1920s* ★☆☆☆☆

Art Deco enameled minaudière with caricature of opera singer Enrico Caruso (1873–1921). Signed "LaCloche Frères Paris," with facsimile of Caruso's signature. *c.1925* ★★★★★

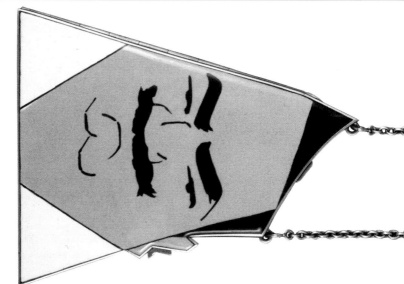

PRECIOUS METALS

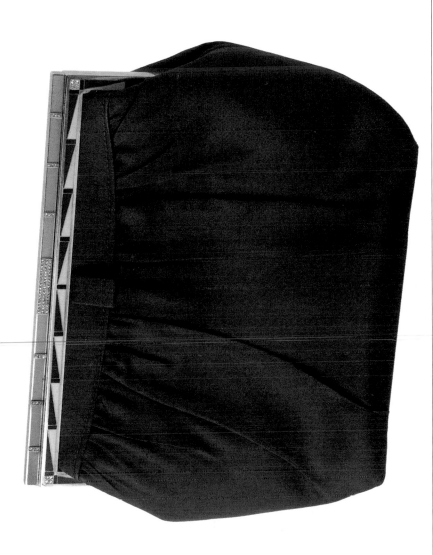

Van Cleef & Arpels Art Deco bag in black silk,
the gold clasp set with enamel and diamonds.
Hallmarked 1925. ★★★★★

Silver finger purse of bombe shape, bright cut, engraved with arabesques; has suspension chain with finger ring. Made by T&S, Chester; initialed. *1919* ★★☆☆☆

Silver finger purse of fan shape, with festoon design and molded edge; has suspension chain and finger ring. Made by BP/DC, Birmingham. *1914* ★ ★ ☆ ☆ ☆

Evening purse of 18-carat woven gold, with hinged flap and mirror inside. ★★★★★

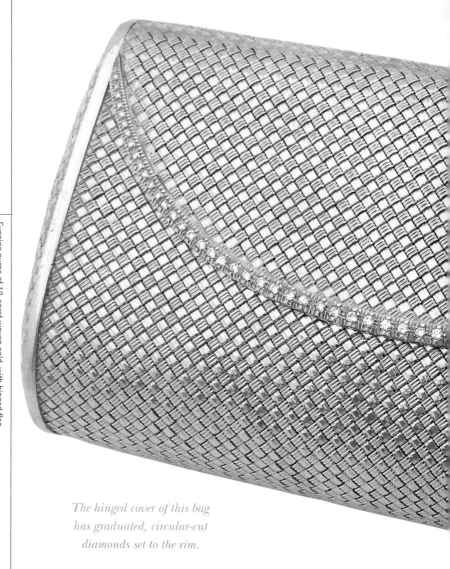

The hinged cover of this bag has graduated, circular-cut diamonds set to the rim.

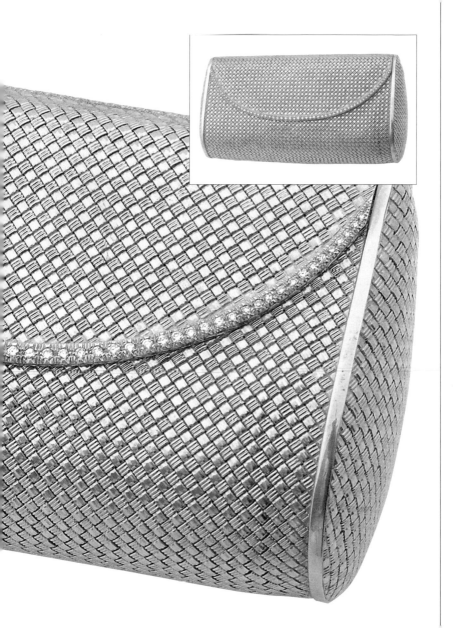

DETAIL: Embossed logo with "K," "EMB," and deer on bag, opposite.

HAND-TOOLED LEATHER BAGS

The Arts and Crafts period of the late 19th and early 20th centuries saw a renewed belief in traditional craftsmanship. This trend led to a rise in the popularity of simple hand-tooled leather bags, which continued into the Art Nouveau period. The bags were made from English or Spanish leather in traditional styles. They often had a fold-over flap, which allowed room for decoration – typically, natural forms such as curling leaves, acorns, and stylized flowers, which appealed to contemporary tastes.

As a reaction against Victorian mass-production and mechanization, bags were hand-made in workshops, often in rural locations. In the United States, many were made at the Roycroft Shops in East Aurora, New York, which housed a group of artists dedicated to working in leather in the style of William Morris. Frederick Kranz and H.E. Kaser Leather Corporation also made hand-tooled bags. The look rather fell out of fashion in the 1930s, although examples are still produced today.

Art Nouveau bag with hand-tooled grape motif; also has embossed logo on body and "Gemco" stamp on frame. *1915* ★★☆☆☆

Alligator-skin handbag with brass hardware. *1920s* ★★☆☆☆

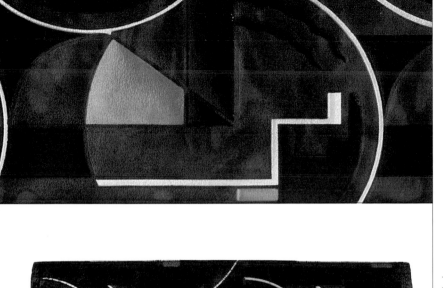

LEATHER

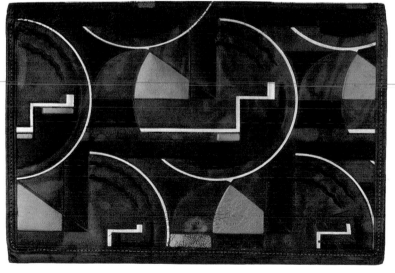

French leather handbag, tooled and stained in shades of brown and black with Art Deco pattern; has silk lining. *c 1925* ★ ★ ☆ ☆

s0261–s0681

French Art Deco bag in black suede, with filigree sterling silver clasp and frame set with marcasite and onyx. Lining has integral change purse. *1920s* ★★★★☆

Tooled and colored leather clutch bag, lined with beige moiré silk. c.1920 ★ ☆☆☆☆

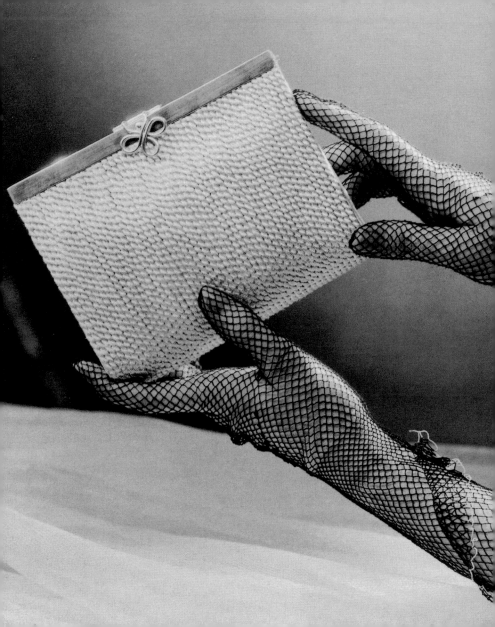

1930s–1940s

From the glamorous geometric styling that is a hallmark of 1930s Art Deco bags to the practical roominess of wartime bags, this was a time of contrasts. Beaded and embroidered bags continued to be popular – especially home-made bags when wartime shortages meant new ones were hard to come by – while box bags made their first appearance.

Anne Marie of France and the Italian designer Elsa Schiaparelli added novel and surreal notes to handbag design, which would echo for years to come.

American hand-beaded and embroidered clutch bag with ivory satin lining and satin-backed mirror; marked "Bags by Josef, Hand beaded in the USA." *1930s* ★☆☆☆☆

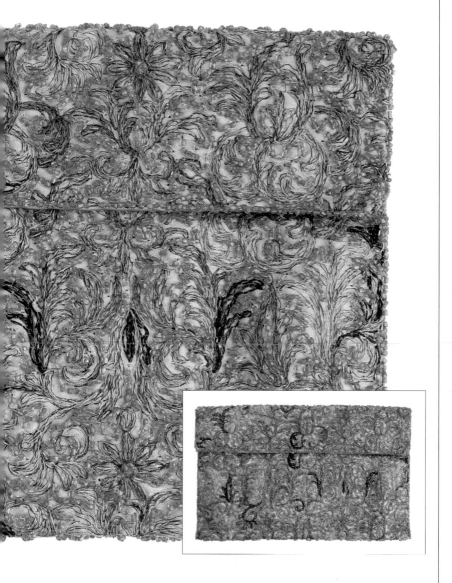

French olive-green satin clutch bag with white and gray beadwork. Lining is marked "Made in France for Coblentz." *1930s* ★ ☆☆☆☆

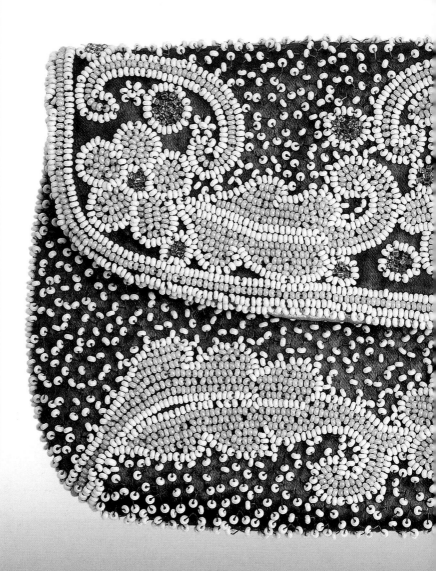

Evening bag with hand-beaded and enameled frame and clasp. Labeled "The French Bag Shop, 1116 Lincoln Road, Miami Beach, Florida." *1930s* ★★★ ★★☆ ☆

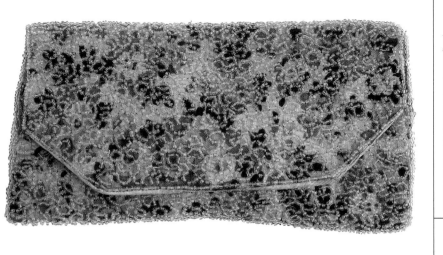

Evening purse with clear beadwork over floral satin. Lining is marked "Made in France, Hand made." *1930s* ★ ☆ ☆ ☆ ☆

Small bag with embroidered flowers on white beaded ground and gilt metal clasp and handle. *1930s* ★ ☆ ☆ ☆ ☆

Beadwork bag with cream and white floral design, beaded clasp and catch, and gilt metal chain strap. Cream silk lining is labeled "K&G Charlet Bag." ★ ☆☆☆☆

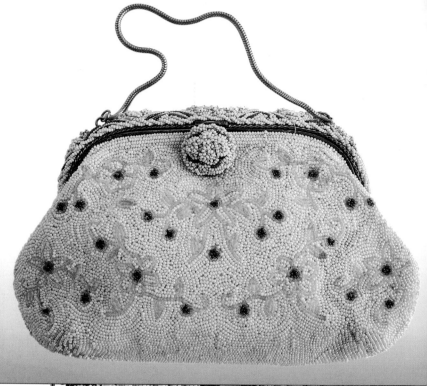

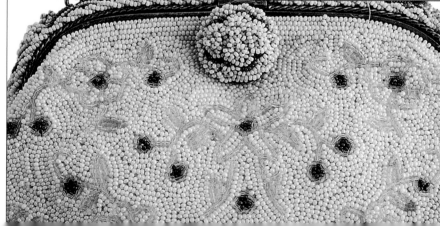

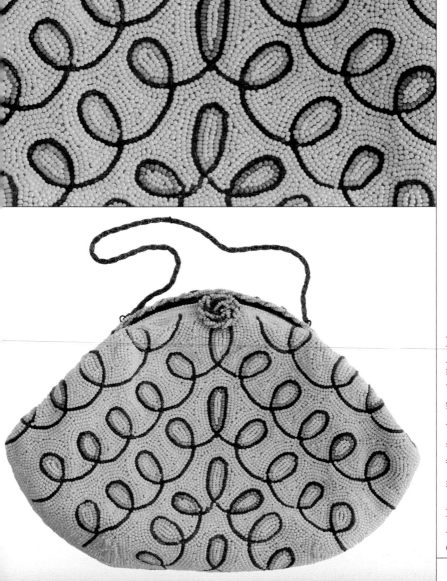

Beadwork bag with curling thread motif, and with beaded catch and clasp. Lining is labeled "Bags by Josef Hand Beaded in France." *1930s* ★ ☆ ☆ ☆

DETAIL: Interior of purse, with compartments and beadwork decoration.

French two-handled cream silk purse with pink, cream, white, sky blue, and metallic beadwork. *1930s* ★☆☆☆☆

Austrian "duffle" handbag with very fine yellow ochre, mint green, amethyst, and rose-pink beads.   *1930s*   ★★★☆☆

Embroidery and beadwork purse with beaded handle, metal frame, and sprung cover. Cream silk lining is labeled "Handmade in Belgium." *1930s* ★ ☆ ☆ ☆

Beaded evening bag with black and silver stripes. *1940s* ★☆☆☆☆

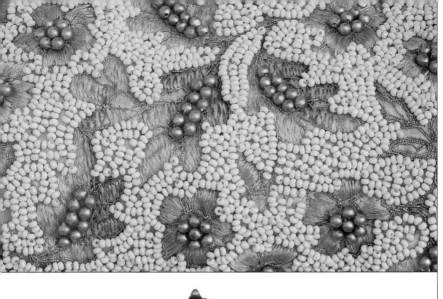

French hand-beaded and embroidered evening purse with pearl decoration. Lining s marked "Jolles Original." *1930s*

☆☆☆☆
★

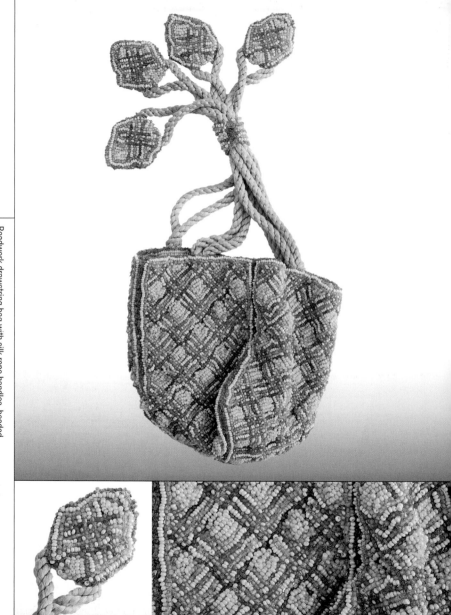

Beadwork drawstring bag with silk rope handles, beaded collar, and tassels. Lining has gilt stamp "Saks Fifth Avenue Made in France." *1930s* ★ ★ ☆ ☆ ☆

Art Deco beadwork bag with peacock design, beaded fringe, and gilt metal clasp and handle. Also has rare leather lining; beaded bags are usually lined with silk. *1930s* ★ ☆ ☆ ☆

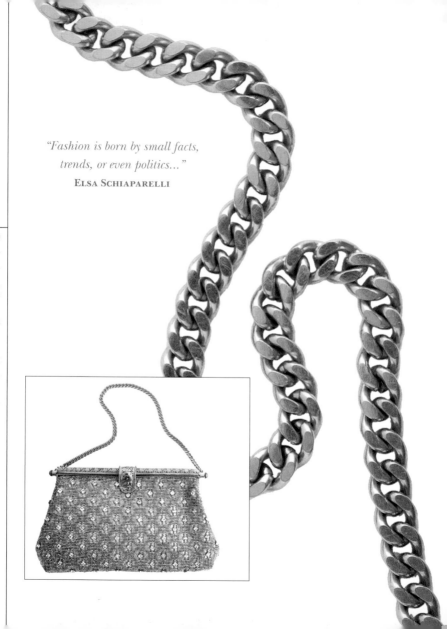

1930s–1940s

"*Fashion is born by small facts, trends, or even politics...*"
ELSA SCHIAPARELLI

Beadwork and diamanté purse with gilt metal clasp and chain strap. White silk lining is labeled "Made in France." *1930s* ★★☆☆☆

DETAIL: Clasp, with fretted pattern and printed porcelain plaque.

p.273

p.271

p.275

p.172

p.146

p.174

p.268

p.229

p.147

p.84

p.400

p.341

p.379

p.409

p.432

p.401

Art Deco beaded bag, in fine condition. *1930s* ★★☆☆☆

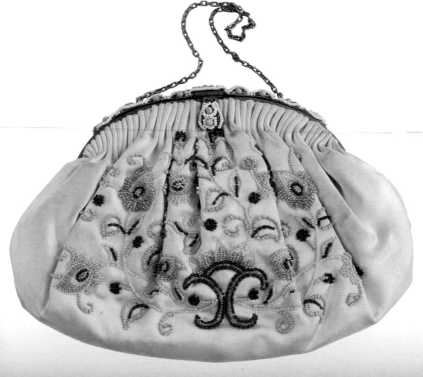

French silk purse with leaf and flower beadwork design and beaded frame and catch. Lining is labeled "Exclusive Handbags by Ed B. Robinson." *1930s* ★ ☆ ☆ ☆ ☆

French clutch bag with gold and colored beadwork and enameled clasp. *1940s* ★★★☆☆

The clasp of this bag is finely decorated with enameled flowers and intricate micro-beading.

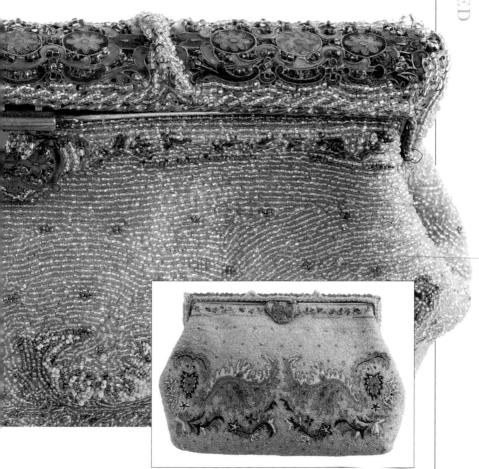

1930s–1940s

French evening bag with gold micro-beading, embroidered detail, beaded and enameled clasp, and gilt chain strap. Interior has satin-backed mirror. Marked "Bag by Josef." *1940s* ★★★☆☆

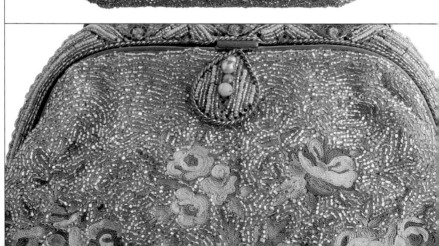

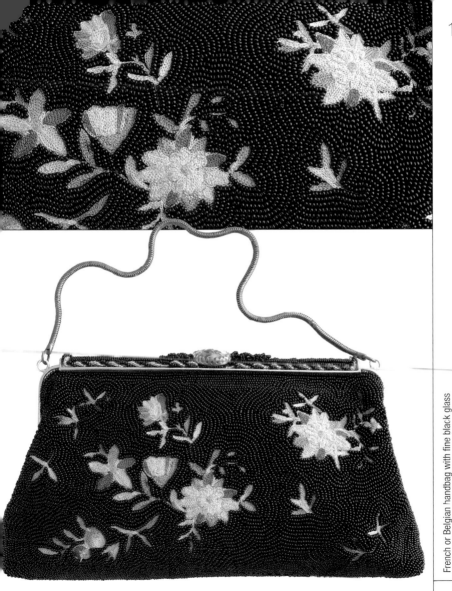

French or Belgian handbag with fine black glass beads and floral motifs; also has gold-plated frame and chain strap. *1940s* ★ ☆☆☆☆

Gold, clear, and white beadwork handbag with beaded clasp and handle. *1930s* ★ ☆ ☆ ☆ ☆

Purse with black basket-weave beadwork, similar
beadwork handle, gilt metal frame with pavé diamanté,
and black silk lining.   1930s   ★ ★ ☆ ☆ ☆

Blue carnival bead box bag with twisted, beaded handle. *1940s* ★☆☆☆☆

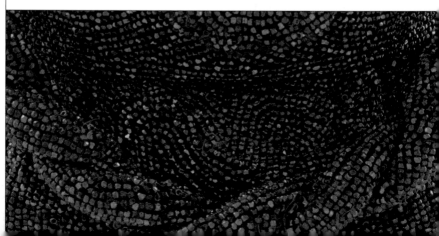

Small French bag with scrolling floral pattern in fine beads. Clasp is silver-plated with porcelain cameo. *1940s* ★★★☆☆

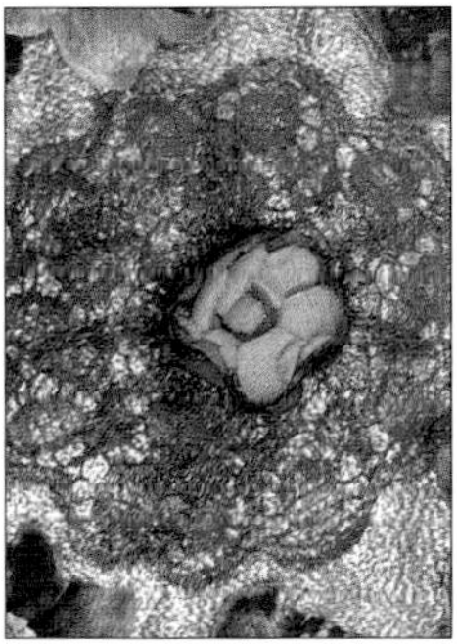

Vintage floral purse with gold lace trim. ★☆☆☆☆

DuBonnette gunmetal beaded box bag with beaded handle and gilt metal clasp. *1940s* ★☆☆☆☆

Garnet-beaded evening bag, with beaded handle and looped gold-tone metal clasp. *1940s* ★★☆☆☆

Evening bag with beaded and painted floral design and gold-tone metal clasp. *1940s* ★★☆☆☆

"Innovation! One cannot be forever innovating. I want to create classics."

COCO CHANEL

French clutch bag with fine glass beads. White metal clasp is set with three faux pearls. *1940s* ★★★☆☆

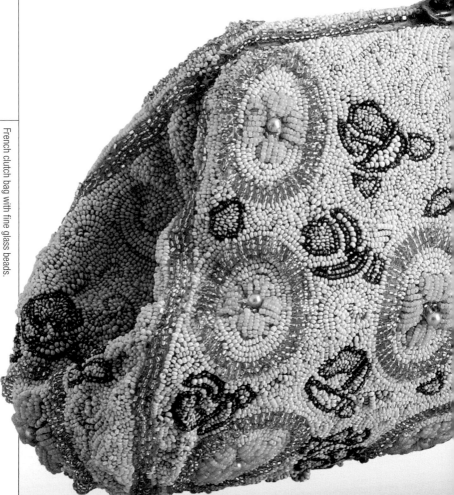

Black silk moiré evening bag with cut steel beads; also has white metal clasp set with paste stones. *1940s* ★★☆☆☆

Black satin, hand-embroidered evening purse with beaded and enameled frame, satin handle, and yellow satin lining; probably French. *1940s* ★ ★ ☆ ☆ ☆

Hand-beaded evening purse with tambour-stitched flowers, beaded frame and clasp, gilt snake chain strap, and black satin coin purse. Marked "Made in France Pierre Marot Paris." Unused. *1940s* ★★☆☆☆

French beaded and embroidered evening bag in moiré silk, with brass closure and chain strap. *1940s* ★ ★ ☆ ☆ ☆

French beaded vanity bag, with lipstick, powder, and cigarette compartments inside. Suitcase bags were extremely rare. ★★★☆☆

"I loathe narcissism, but I approve of vanity."

DIANA VREELAND

Black beadwork bag with figural design and
beaded handle. *1940s* ★★★☆☆

Black beadwork bag with embroidered
floral design. *1940s* ★★☆☆☆

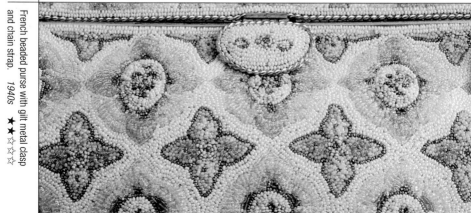

French beaded purse with gilt metal clasp and chain strap. *1940s* ★★☆☆☆

Clutch bag with copper-colored beads in ribbed pattern; also has etched gilt metal clasp and frame. *1940s* ★★☆☆

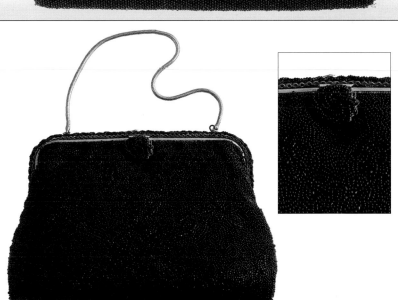

French handbag with fine black glass beads, brass frame, and snake chain strap. *Late 1940s* ★★☆☆

FLOWER POWER

p.328

p.345

p.283

p.277

p.355

p.361

p.30

p.49

p.59

p.60 p.145 p.180

p.322 p.159 p.317

p.303 p.360 p.417

FLOWER POWER

White beaded bag with figural design, gilt metal clasp, and beaded handle. *1940s* ★★★☆☆

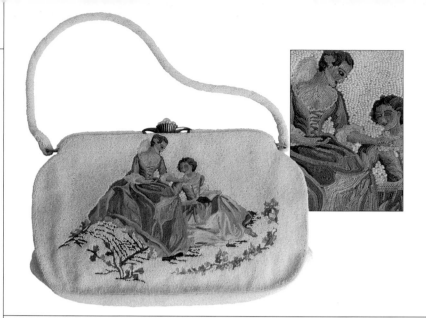

French or Belgian clutch bag with fine black and polychrome beadwork and gold-plated frame. *1940s* ★★☆☆☆

DETAIL: Plaque with its figural decoration.

Black crêpe bag with gold metal clasp and porcelain-effect plaque surrounded by rhinestones. *1940s* ★★☆☆☆

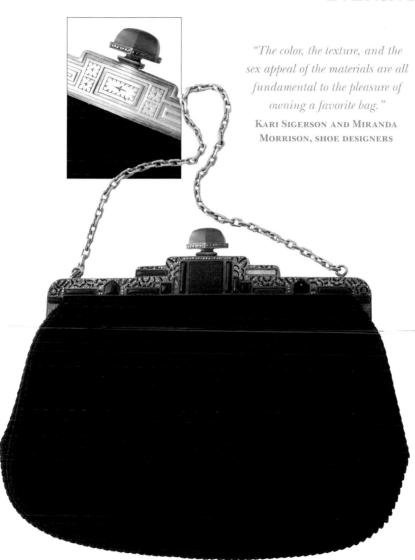

"*The color, the texture, and the sex appeal of the materials are all fundamental to the pleasure of owning a favorite bag.*"

KARI SIGERSON AND MIRANDA MORRISON, SHOE DESIGNERS

Art Deco bag of pleated black silk, with replaced chain. Silver frame is set with carnelian, onyx, and marcasite and has European hallmarks. ★ ☆ ☆ ☆

Velvet opera bag by Chevalier, Paris; has three compartments to hold opera glasses, make up, and a purse. ★☆☆☆☆

Small black silk evening bag with gilt metal chain strap.
Clasp is gilt metal with enameling, beads and faux
pearls.   *1940s*   ★ ★ ☆ ☆ ☆

American gold mesh bag with brass frame, chain strap, and rhinestone-decorated clasp; labeled "Whiting & Davis Co. Mesh Bags." c.1940 ★ ☆☆☆☆

French bag in black suede, with suede strap. Gilt metal clasp is set with eramel and rhinestones Cream satin interior has small purse attached. *1940s* ★★☆☆

FRE-MOR

In the 1940s, Fre-Mor was renowned for its range of beaded bags. The bags were made in various shapes, such as round, rectangular, and hexagonal, with gilt metal frames and silk linings.

Today, collectors will pay a premium for round or rectangular bags. In addition, they look for bags with intricate frames or frames set with Bakelite, both of which add to the value. Also sought after are bags decorated with iridescent "carnival" glass beads. Similar bags were made by companies such as DuBonnette.

The owners of Fre-Mor Plastics later merged with Jewel Plastics Corp. to form Llewellyn, Inc. The Llewellyn company is best known for its Lucite handbags, produced during the 1950s.

Fre-Mor box bag with bronze-colored beads, twisted beadwork handle, gilt metal frame, and f¹ve internal compartments. *1940s* ★★☆☆☆

French clutch bag in black suede. Gilt metal clasp is set with beads in a Paisley pattern and has small enamel cameo. *Early 1930s* ★★★☆☆

Fre-Mor box bag with black beadwork, twisted beadwork handle, and silver-tone metal surround; has five internal compartments. *1940s* ★★☆☆☆

Navy crêpe bag with crêpe handle and gold ring clasp; marked "Gail's Original." Antiqued gold frame is set with gems in a floral motif. *1940s* ★★★☆☆

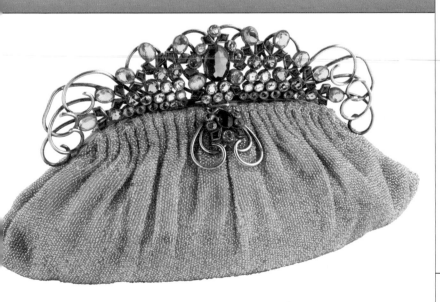

Beaded clutch bag by Josef, with exuberant gilt metal and beaded clasp. ★★★☆☆

Hand-stitched needlework bag in mint condition. Also has engraved silver frame, clasp set with marcasites, and chain strap.   *1930s*   ★★★☆☆

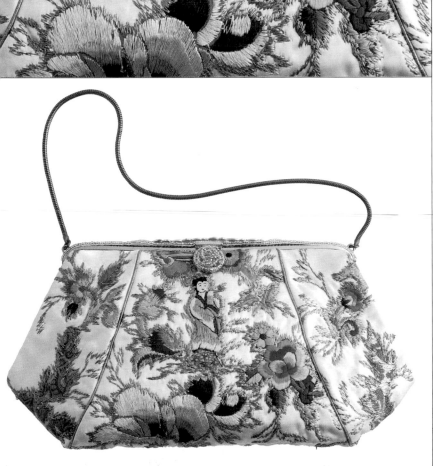

Silk-satin bag by Krucker of London, with embroidery and appliqué in gold and silk, and enameled frame. Comes with booklet explaining symbolism of design. *1940s* ★★★☆☆

LINES AND CURVES

p.265

p.264

p.239

p.217

p.372

p.377

p.195

p.166

p.396

p.210

p.175

p.208

p.190

p.189

p.194

p.336

LINES AND CURVES

American handbag in green wicker and floral-print cotton, with drawstring top. *c.1935* ★☆☆☆☆

Guild Creations wool bag with zip closure. Wave-shaped metal frame is engraved with small flowers and set with paste stones. *1940s* ★★☆☆☆

The Russian-born designer Sonia Delaunay worked in Paris. Her geometric patterns, with colors partly inspired by Russian patchwork, were a great influence on the Art Deco movement.

Art Deco embroidered handbag, in the style of Sonia Delaunay. ★★☆☆☆

Tapestry bag, probably French. *1930s* ★ ☆ ☆ ☆

"Duffle" handbag, probably American, of striped silk with embroidered flowers, ivorine frame, and carved ivorine clasp. *Early 1930s* ★ ★ ☆ ☆

DETAIL: "Champagne bucket" label on front of bag.

ANNE MARIE

Witty and slightly surreal, the remarkable bags by Anne Marie of Paris are avidly collected today. Forms included everything from pianos to telephones and clocks to powder puffs. Great emphasis was also placed on the functional aspects of the bag; openings and fastenings, such as the "roll-top" lid on a desk-shaped bag, were often an integral part of the themed design. Anne Marie used materials, such as Lucite, that were new and innovative and created a playful look, while the black suede used on many bags ensured a glamorous feel.

One notable example of Anne Marie's work is a 1930s bag shaped as a mandolin, complete with "strings," and an interior decorated with an opera program. Another is a striking 1940s bag shaped as an ice bucket, with Lucite "ice" and a bottle of Reims champagne, which was made as a Christmas gift for VIP residents of the Ritz Hotel, Paris.

Champagne bucket bag by Anne Marie of Paris: black buckskin with clear Lucite "ice cube" lid and gold-plated trim. *1940s* ★★★★

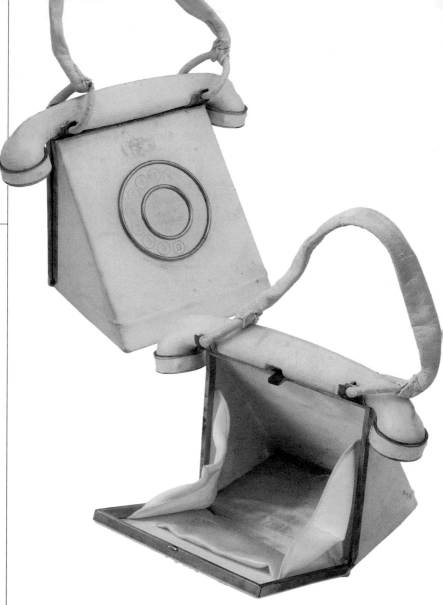

Extremely rare surreal telephone handbag, in white kid leather, by Anne Marie of Paris. *1940s* ★★★★☆

Anne Marie of Paris playing cards bag: buckskin with gold motifs and ivory dice clasp. *1940s* ★★★★☆

Anne Marie of Paris telephone bag of black buckskin with gilt frame. Made as a gift for VIPs at the Ritz Hotel, Paris. *1940s* ★★★★★

1930s–1940s

Bucket bag with Bakelite lid, bronze beading to body and handle, and gilt metal catch. Lid has mirror set inside it. *1940s* ★★☆☆☆

☆☆☆
★★

French Lucite purse decorated with gold beads. *1940s*

American handbag with
voile body and butterscotch
Bakelite frame. *1940s* ★★☆☆☆

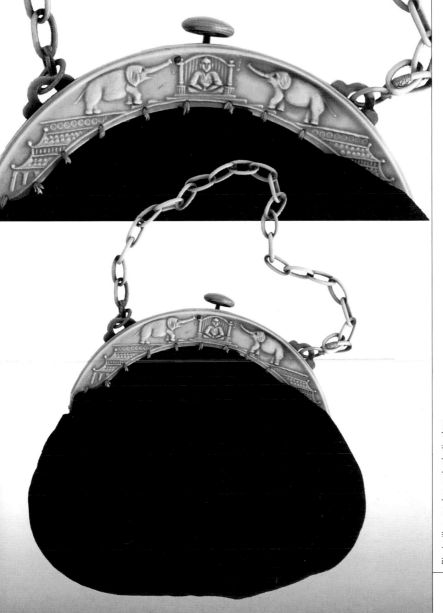

Black silk purse: has early plastic clasp, with molded elephant design, and plastic chain strap. *c.1930* ★☆☆☆☆

DETAIL: Colored inlays on body of bag.

ART DECO BAKELITE BAG

In the 1920s and 1930s, plastic was an exciting new material that opened a world of possibilities to designers of handbags, jewelry, and other accessories. Bakelite was a form of plastic patented by Dr. Leo Baekeland in 1907. It was initially used as an electrical insulator, but was soon living up to its reputation as "the material of 1,000 uses." As well as being colorful, Bakelite was easy to carve into intricate and highly decorative shapes.

The Art Deco bag featured on these pages shows the many possibilities Bakelite brought to handbag design. The creamy yellow body has been inlaid with pieces of red, green, and black Bakelite. In addition, the bag has a Bakelite handle and clasp.

Art Deco Bakelite purse: cream inlaid with red, green, and black stylized floral design. *1930s* ★★★☆☆

Black silk evening bag with Bakelite and diamanté clasp. *c.1930* ★★☆☆☆

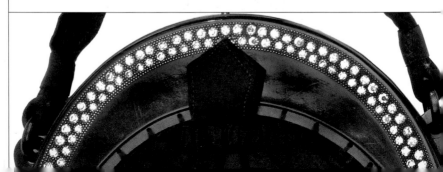

Silk purse with celluloid rose clasp. This
purse is rare.   *1930s*

★★ ☆☆
★★

Brazilian ponyskin bag by Aveda, with hand-stitched detail and clear Lucite and brass clasp. *1940s* ★★☆☆☆

DETAIL: Suede change purse inside bag.

PAB. DE BOLSAS
S. SOHEIN
IND. BRASILEIRA
Coelho Netto

Black calfskin handbag by Bogan, USA, with accordion top and recessed base. Green satin lining retains original patent tag. *Late 1940s* ★★★☆☆

Black leather faux crocodile clutch bag with red leather interior. *1940s* ★ ☆ ☆ ☆ ☆

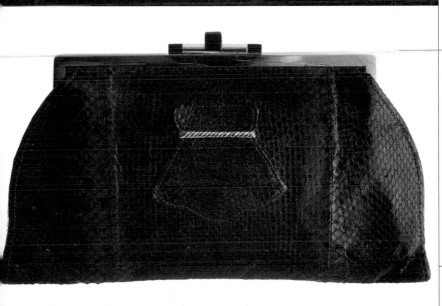

☆☆☆☆☆ ★

1940s

Python-skin purse with fitted interior.

SCHIAPARELLI

One of the most influential designers of the 20th century, Elsa Schiaparelli (1890–1973) was known for radical and witty clothing inspired by modern and surrealist art. Her handbags, like her other accessories, were often created from new, man-made materials in striking colors and forms. Examples from the 1930s included bags shaped as snails and balloons, or made from newsprint fabric or Cellophane. One flamboyant handbag featured a telephone and was created with the help of the artist Salvador Dali. Despite such innovation, many of her bags were feminine and classically stylish and worked well with more conventional outfits.

Schiaparelli also worked on themed ranges. Handbags in her 1937 "Music" collection played tunes when opened, while her "Pagan" bags were decorated with suede leaves. Always keen to attract publicity with groundbreaking and practical bags for modern women, Schiaparelli continued to make handbags into the 1950s.

Schiaparelli bag in black calfskin, with gilt metal clasp; made in Italy. *1930s* ★★★ ★★☆☆

British Art Deco bag with stitched geometric design and white metal frame. *c.1930* ★★☆☆☆

Brown leather accordion handbag by Milch,
USA, with gilt metal hardware and maker's
mark. *1940s–1950s* ★★☆☆☆

Argentinian brown crocodile-skin bag, with two handles and gold-tone hardware, marked "Industria Argentina." *1940s* ★★☆☆☆

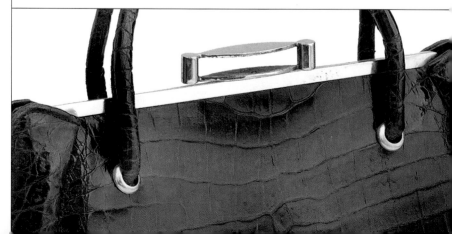

Crocodile-skin bag with black leather lining and gilt clasp. The good condition of this bag increases its desirability. *1940s* ★ ★ ☆ ☆ ☆

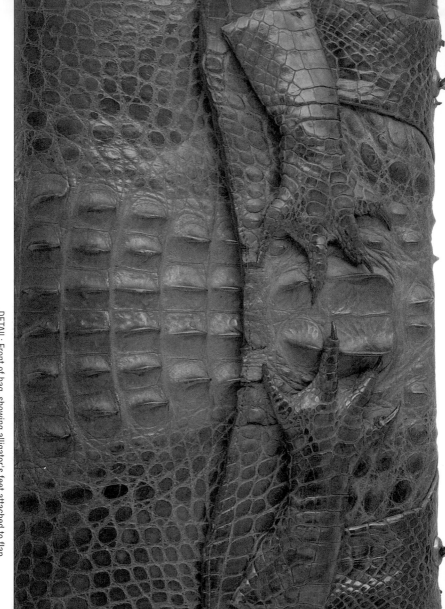

DETAIL: Front of bag, showing alligator's feet attached to flap.

THE CLASSIC ALLIGATOR BAG

Relatively early in the history of handbags, designs began to appear in exotic animal skins such as python, antelope, and shark. It was alligator skin, however, that really captured the fashion world's imagination.

Alligator bags enjoyed their first wave of popularity during the 1880s, when Bloomingdale's offered them for sale in all shapes and sizes. The commercial success of the material led to manufacturers introducing "faux" alligator bags made from grained goatskin.

In the 1930s the craze went one step further, with designers using the whole animal to create a bag. These examples – which can feature the creature's head and feet – are not to everyone's taste today, but are still highly collectable. During the 1950s, Hermès used alligator skin for its famous "Kelly" bag. Two alligators were used for each bag: the belly formed the bag's body, while the flexible neck skin was used for the sides.

★★☆☆☆

Alligator-skin handbag with brass hardware. 1930s

Lizardskin clutch bag with brass clasps, by Picard, West Germany. *1940s* ★★☆☆☆

Argentinian brown crocodile-skin handbag, marked "Industria Argentina." *1930s* ★★☆☆☆

"A good handbag is something one can afford to be snobbish about; it is so very much a sign of good breeding."

**DORA SHACKELL,
ACCENT ON ACCESSORIES**

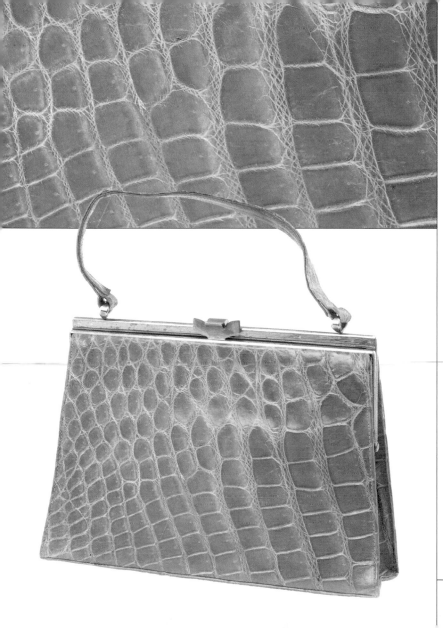

Honey-colored crocodile-skin handbag.
Mid-1930s ★ ☆☆☆☆

Small Art Deco-style suedette bag, with pleated geometric pattern, suedette handle, and domed brass clasp.   *1940s*   ★ ★ ☆ ☆ ☆

French bag in black lizardskin, with enameled and cut steel frame and cha n strap. *1930s* ★★★★☆

Red snakeskin bag with gilt metal hardware.   *1940s*   ★★☆☆☆

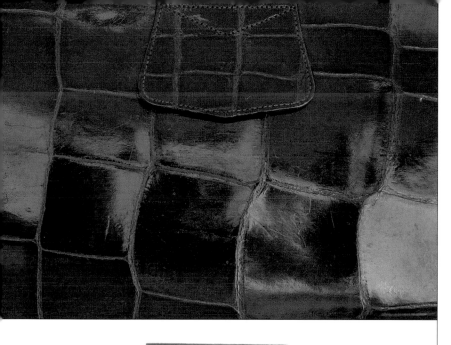

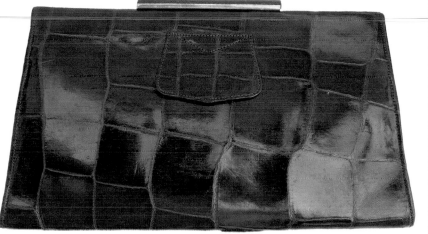

Brown crocodile-skin clutch bag, marked "British Made." *1930s* ☆☆☆ ★☆

1950s–1960s

The post-war boom brought with it a new informality in fashion. While baskets and novelty shapes suited both the optimism of the 1950s and the flower power of the 1960s, formal, classy, coordinating leather bags were still a necessity.

Perhaps the 1950s' greatest legacy to handbag design was the Lucite bag – a plastic box bag that came in myriad colours and designs. After years in the style wilderness, these masterpieces of modern design are now appreciated and collected as icons of their time.

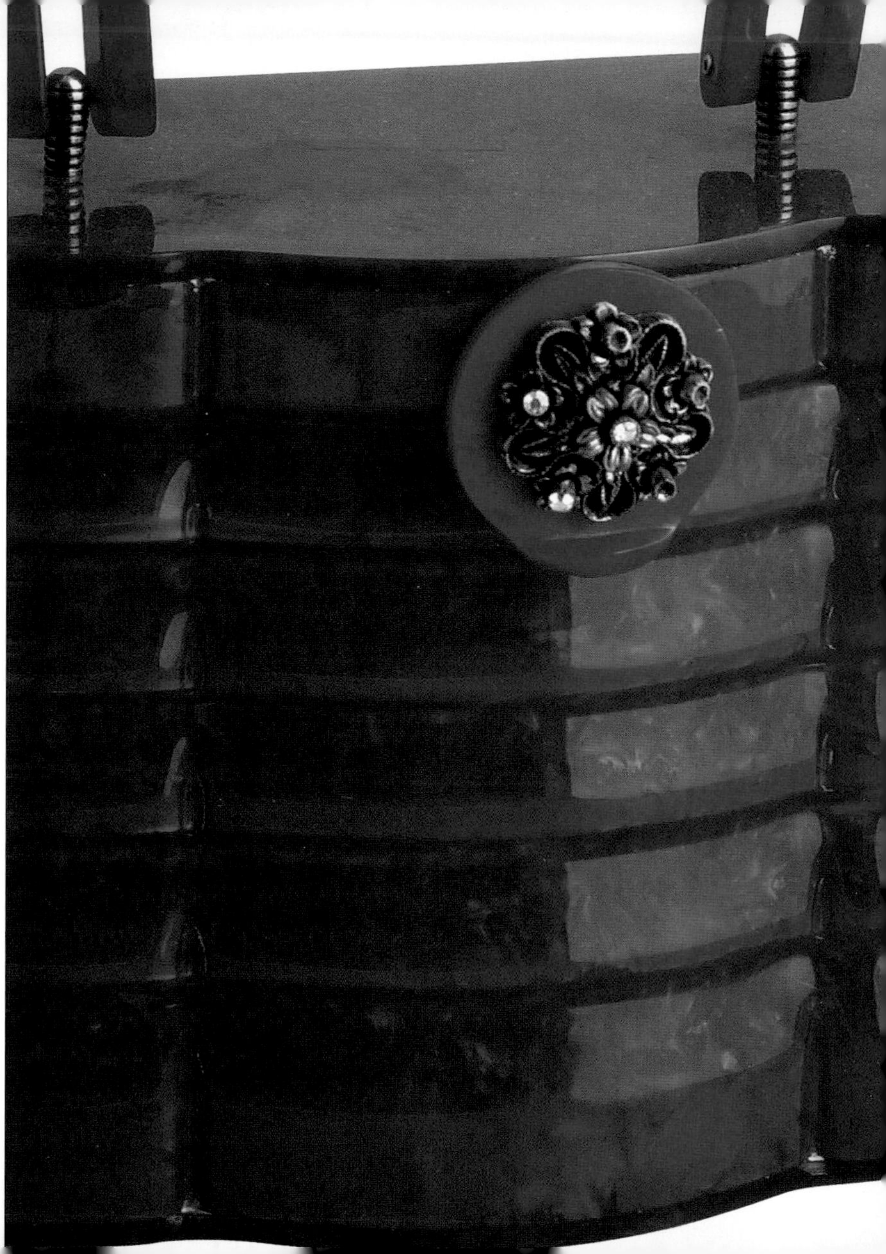

THE CLASSIC LUCITE BAG

By the early 1950s, plastic had become ubiquitous in American homes. Meanwhile, innovative handbag manufacturers started using a tough plastic, trademarked Lucite, developed in the 1930s. For many women in the emerging middle classes, leather and fabric bags were too expensive; Lucite bags, though hand-made, were affordable and their novelty shapes fitted with post-war optimism. By the end of the decade, however, the availability of cheap, mass-produced bags, combined with a return to the fashion for leather, caused the Lucite craze to die out.

The major manufacturers were Myles Originals, Gilli Originals, Wilardy Originals, Llewellyn, Inc., Tyrolean, Inc., Rialto, Dorset Rex, Charles S Khan, Maxim, Majestic, Miami, and Florida Handbags. Most bags were labeled.

When buying Lucite bags, condition is important; cracks, or deterioration such as fogging, will reduce the value.

Sculptured red Lucite purse, the clasp decorated with rhinestones. *1950s* ★★ ★★★★

Marbleized silver Lucite bag, with carved leaf design, double handles, scrolling initials "RJG" to lid, and clear Lucite feet. *1950s* ★★☆☆☆

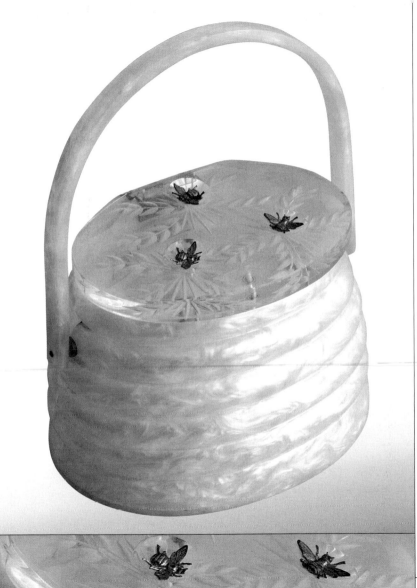

American "Beehive" handbag, with body of ribbed and pearlized white Lucite, and top of clear Lucite with inset gold-plated bee motifs. *1950s* ★★★☆☆

Black Lucite handbag by Wiesner set with a band of pearls and rhinestones around base. *Early 1950s* ★★★★☆

American handbag with brass frame and clasp and black Lucite body inset with abstract brass motifs. *1950s* ★★★☆☆

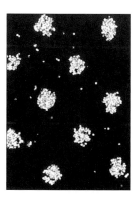

Basket-shaped Lucite purse with wavy ruff and gilt metal hardware. *1950s* ★ ★ ☆ ☆ ☆

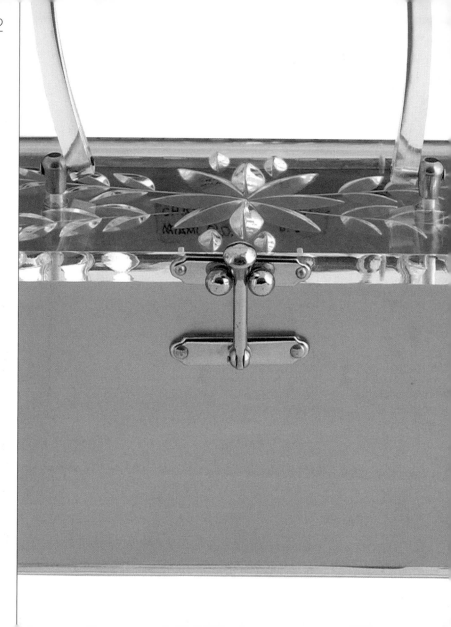

CHARLES S KHAN

Lucite bags by Charles S Khan are often a solid, metallic color – pink, blue, or gold – with clear lids and handles. Both the lids and the handles can feature geometric or floral cut designs. Other bags feature clear or white Lucite set with gold confetti. Charles S Khan used the three-ball catch favored by Patricia of Miami and Myles Originals.

Like many of its competitors, Charles S Khan made the same style of bag in many colorways and different shapes – oval, rectangular, circular, and trapezoid.

The company was based in Miami, Florida. Bags are usually labeled "Charles S Khan, Inc. Miami," or "Charles S Khan, Inc. Miami, Florida, USA."

Turquoise Lucite handbag by Charles S Khan, with clear lid and handles and white metal hardware. This bag is valuable because turquoise is a rare color for a Lucite bag. *Early 1950s* ★★★★☆

Shiny satin white Lucite handbag by Charles S Khan of Miami, Florida. Clear lid has a molded criss-cross design. *Early 1950s* ★★☆☆☆

Florida silver Lucite handbag with white metal clasp. *Mrd-1950s* ★★☆☆☆

DETAIL: Dorset Rex manufacturer's mark.

DORSET REX

Clever combinations of metal and plastic are the signature of Dorset Rex's bags. The company often used a metal filigree, mesh, or basketweave for the body of a bag and gave it a plastic base, lid, and handle. The metal would be white or yellow, and the plastic parts might be black, taupe, or tortoiseshell.

Other basket styles had alternating ribs of plastic and metal, while some bags were barrel-shaped and made entirely from plastic but with a metal overlay around the bottom half of the body.

Dorset Rex also made other unusual designs, such as clear plastic baskets in which the plastic was inset with plastic flowers, and imitation mother-of-pearl evening bags.

Lucite bag by Dorset Rex 5th Avenue, with gilt metal panel and ball feet and clear Lucite handle. *1950s* ★★☆☆☆

Woven metal handbag by Dorset Rex 5th Avenue, with plastic lid and red lining. *Early 1950s* ★ ☆☆☆☆

Majestic clear Lucite confetti bag with gilt metal frame and hardware. Clear bags were often lined with fabric to match the wearer's dress. *1950s* ★ ☆ ☆ ☆

White and gilt metal woven box bag. *1950* ★ ☆ ☆ ☆

DETAIL: Decorative disk set with pearls and rhinestones.

LLEWELLYN, INC.

The Lucite bags made by Llewellyn, Inc. are elegant and understated. They are often decorated with rhinestones or lined with satin. Llewellyn, Inc. bags may also have ornate metal clasps or inset decoration such as monogram initials or intricate filigree.

The company, which was based on Madison Avenue in New York City, was formed in 1951 when Jewel Plastic Corp. and Fre-Mor Manufacturing Corp. merged. Its trademark was "Lewsid Jewel by Llewellyn." Some designs, such as the beehive bag with its jeweled lid engraved with bees and flowers, were made by both Jewel Plastic Corp. and Llewellyn, Inc.

Most of the Llewellyn, Inc. bags found today have carrying handles; clutch bags are rare and therefore command a premium.

Lucite Llewellyn handbag, with looped handle and silver tone metal hardware. *Mid-1950s* ★★★☆☆

Rare gray shell Lucite handbag by Llewellyn, Inc., with twisted handles. *1950s* ★★★★☆

Mottled gray Lucite bag with circular handle. Also has moiré silk lining; with internal pockets   1950s   ★ ★ ☆ ☆ ☆

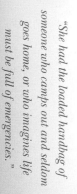

"She had the loaded handbag of someone who camps out and seldom goes home, or who imagines life must be full of emergencies."

MAVIS GALLANT, CANADIAN WRITER

Black Lucite purse with fitted interior, compartments, and mirror. *1950s* ★★★☆☆

American "casket" handbag with black Lucite body, "gold pin" decoration, and clear, carved Lucite lid. *1950s* ★ ★ ☆ ☆

Black straw purse with wooden lid; has Lucite panel with goldfish design. *1950s* ★ ★ ☆ ☆

DETAIL: Clear plastic lid, hand-carved with rose and leaf design.

MYLES ORIGINALS

The Lucite bags made by Myles Originals can often be identified by their metal, three-ball clasps. As with the bags made by other manufacturers, the more intricate the bag, the greater its value. Inset diamanté gems, fancy clasps, internal trays, and mirrors all add to the desirability of a bag. Color also has an impact on a bag's collectability. Black, brown, white, and pearlized gray are all common colors; red, pale blue, jade green, and yellow are all rare.

When buying a Lucite bag, check that it does not smell strongly of chemicals. If it does, it means the plastic is degrading and will start to crack and discolor. Bags should not be subjected to high temperatures or left in direct sunlight for long periods.

Caramel-colored Lucite handbag by Myles Originals, with striated butterscotch body and handles, clear lid, and gilt metal catch. *Early 1950s* ★ ★ ★ ☆ ☆

Handbag by Myles Originals: clear Lucite set with copper and silver threads, and with silver-tone metal catch and feet. *Early 1950s* ★★☆☆☆

Butterscotch Lucite handbag by Myles Originals, with white metal hardware. *Early 1950s* ★★☆☆

Caramel-colored Lucite bag with waffle-carved body and apple juice-colored lid; maker unknown. *Mid-1950s* ★★☆☆

DETAIL: Avocado-green body with gold and green confetti spots.

PATRICIA OF MIAMI

This line of elegant Lucite handbags was named by Morty Edelstein, head of Miami Handbags, in honor of his wife Patricia. Morty Edelstein had previously worked for Fre-Mor and Llewellyn in New York before joining Miami Handbags in Florida.

The bags often feature solid-colored bodies and cut, clear Lucite lids with the three-ball metal clasps also seen on Myles Originals and Charles S Khan bags. Patricia of Miami's distinctive designs include elongated box bags with two openings separated by a band of filigree metal; bags made from clear Lucite with gold threads set inside it, gold with gold threads, or gray with silver threads; and bags made from Lucite set with lace or glitter. Evening bags were set with rhinestones. The bags were often marked "Patricia of Miami."

Patricia of M ami bag with racecar-style body, clear Lucite lid with hand-carved decoration, and ball feet. *Mid-1950s* ★ ★ ☆ ☆ ☆

Handbag by Shoreham: clear Lucite encasing stripes of silver confetti and threads and blue confetti with mother-of-pearl pieces. *1950s*   ★★★☆☆

Handbag by Shoreham, unsigned: glitter Lucite with gray and silver confetti, and set with rhinestones at base of handle. *Mid-1950s*   ★★★☆☆

Silver and clear Lucite wedding handbag, unsigned. Lid can be removed so that flowers or other decorations can be placed inside. *1950s* ★ ★ ★ ☆ ☆

RIALTO

Lucite bags embellished with cut designs, or with applied jewels or flowers, are the hallmarks of the Rialto company. Cut designs often featured flowers, heart-shaped leaves, stars, or geometric patterns. Applied flowers would be made from fabric, threads, and beads. Rialto bags often feature the company's signature "stirrup and turn" style latch. They may be marked "Rialto Original, NY."

Some Rialto box bags were covered with acetate sleeves. Other box bags were actually made from acetate; these are often confused with the Lucite bags. Telling the difference can be a challenge to the inexperienced eye, but acetate tends to look slightly yellow when compared to Lucite.

As well as Lucite bags, Rialto made fabric handbags, which were decorated with floral designs and had vinyl coverings.

Pearlized, bone-colored Lucite handbag by Rialto, set with an amber and aurora rhinestone disk. *1950s* ★★★★☆

Pearl-white Rialto handbag with aurora borealis and milk-glass rhinestone decoration. *Mid-1950s* ★★★★☆

Gray Fialto handbag with clear handle and
hand-carved lid. *Early 1950s* ★★☆☆

TYROLEAN, INC.

Bags made by Tyrolean, Inc. of New York are always distinctive. The company's designers favored classic box and cylinder shapes embellished with panels of intricate metal filigree. As well as gilt metal clasps, the bags usually have gilt metal feet and other hardware.

The majority of Tyrolean's bags were made from brown tortoiseshell-effect Lucite, sometimes with clear Lucite lids. Other colors include gray, cream, and white, although bags with blue Lucite panels are known. The bags are usually marked "Tyrolean."

The company also made leather and clear plastic bags with gilt metal frames. One of the most innovative was a pyramid-shaped leather wrist purse with three compartments marked "W," "P," and "C," possibly standing for "wallet," "purse," and "cigarettes" or "cosmetics."

Basket-shaped Lucite bag by Tyrolean Inc., with gilt metal filigree decoration, frame, and clasp. *Mid-1950s* ★ ★ ☆ ☆ ☆

Tortoiseshell Lucite handbag by Tyrolean, Inc., with faux pearls and white metal lid. *Mid-1950s* ★★☆☆☆

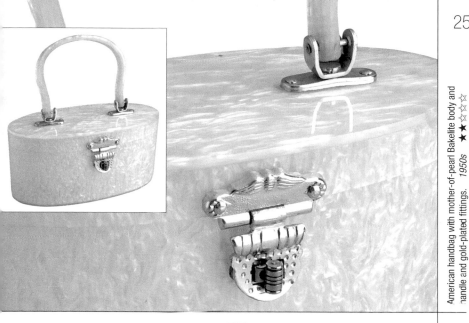

American handbag with mother-of-pearl Bakelite body and handle and gold-plated fittings. *1950s* ★★☆☆☆

Yellow Lucite bag with clear Lucite lid. *1950s* ★★☆☆☆

WILARDY

The revolutionary appearance, the futuristic material, the solid, practical shape: nothing epitomizes 1950s handbag design better than Lucite box bags, and few firms were as influential as Wilardy of New York.

Will Hardy (he used an amalgamation of his names for his line of bags) joined his father's handbag firm in 1948 and immediately concentrated on the production of hardwearing Lucite bags. Shapes were radical and boldly geometric with gentle curves and lollipop handles. Although a man-made material, the plastic made his handbags expensive, as each example was cast and soldered by hand. Rhinestones, glass, and filigree work finished the exteriors and increased the level of exclusivity, making the bags popular with socialites and celebrities.

The invention of injection molding, however, enabled manufacturers to mass-produce plastic items cheaply; as a result, Wilardy soon lost out to competitors and the Lucite box lost its position as the must-have bag of the decade.

Caramel-colored Lucite handbag by Wilardy. This design won an International Fashion Institute design award in 1954. *1950s* ★★★☆☆

Black Lucite handbag by Wilardy, the base of the handle and the clasp set with aurora borealis rhinestones. *Late 1950s* ★★★☆☆

Lucite handbag by Wilardy, decorated with shells, pearls, and tiny gray beads. *1950s* ★★★☆☆

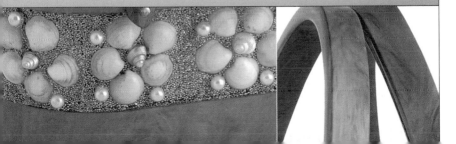

Caramel-colored Lucite handbag by Wilardy, with fitted compact inside lid and gilt metal hardware. *Mid-1950s* ★★★☆☆

Oval-shaped Wilardy handbag of caramel-colored Lucite with pie'ced gilt metal overlay. *Early 1950s* ★★☆☆☆

Blue pearl Luc te handbag by Wilardy, the lid inset with shells, pearls, and beads. This bag is valuable because blue Lucite is rare. *Mid-1950s* ★★★☆☆

Black Lucite handbag by Wilardy, the sides decorated with bands of rhinestones. *Early 1950s* ★★★★☆

Wilardy suitcase bag: black Lucite with hand-painted design representing cities, and gilt metal hardware. The suitcase bags were very popular in the *1950s*. ★★★☆☆

Pearl gray Lucite "bean pot" handbag by Wilardy, the clasp and base of the handle set with rhinestones. *1950s* ★ ★ ★ ☆ ☆

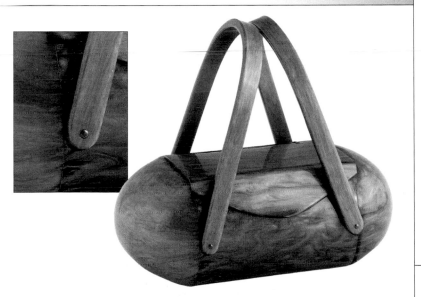

Lucite handbag by Wilardy. This bag was nicknamed "the rocket" because of its shape. *Mid-1950s* ★ ★ ★ ☆ ☆

Caramel-colored Lucite concertina handbag by Wilardy, with three drawers and gilt metal hardware. *Early 1950s* ★★★☆☆

"I added two handles to a hard plastic jewelry box and it looked great as a bag, so I took it from there."
WILL HARDY, HANDBAG DESIGNER

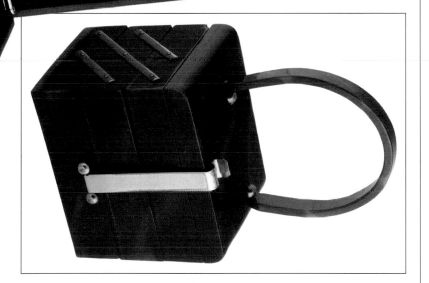

Pink fabric-covered Lucite handbag by Wilardy, with rhinestone leaf design and faux pearls. *1950s* ★★☆☆☆

Pearl-white Lucite handbag by Wilardy with pleated design and black lining. *Late 1950s* ★★★☆☆

Pearl-white, iridescent Lucite handbag by Wilardy, with gold tone metal and rhinestone clasp. This bag was in Will Hardy's private collection. *Late 1950s* ★★★☆☆

Pearl-white Lucite hip bag by Wilardy, with gilt metal and rhinestone decoration on lid and clasp. This is a rare shape. *Late 1950s* ★★★★☆

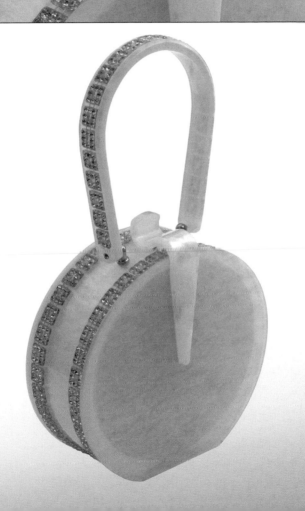

Lucite hatbox-design handbag by Wilardy, the sides and handle set with rhinestones   *Early 1950s*   ★★★☆

LUCITE MASTERS

p.249

p.253

p.250

p.257

p.260

p.256

p.236

p.221

p.239

p.262

p.246

p.245

p.238

p.247

p.231

p.255

p.232

p.258

LUCITE MASTERS

Wooden box bag with Lucite handle; decorated with purple velvet grapes, and lined with brocade and ribbon. Hand-made by "Susan." *1950s* ★☆☆☆☆

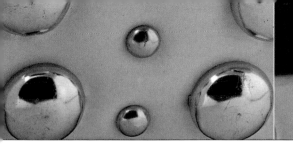

Mod bag with wooden body, white vinyl, and gold bosses; red fabric interior's labeled "Hand-made in British Hong Kong." *1960s* ★ ☆☆☆☆

The hand-painted design shows a scene of "dining doggies."

Painted wooden box bag. Interior has a mirror and is labeled "Collectors Item by Gary Jolie Dallas Decorated for you Made in Hong Kong." *1960s* ★☆☆☆☆

Wooden box bag painted with strawberries and white flowers. *1960s* ★ ☆☆☆

Octagonal wooden handbag with butterfly découpage and Lucite handle. *1950s* ★ ☆☆☆☆

Unusual wooden box handbag with brass handle and
hardware; probably French. *1960s*   ★ ★ ☆ ☆

ENID COLLINS

Established in 1959 in Texas, the Enid Collins company was known for producing unusual, distinctive box bags that continue to win a huge number of fans today. Rectangular in shape, and solidly made from wood, the bags were sturdy and hardwearing, and each was finished to a high standard. Sequins, paint, and faux jewels adorned the flat surfaces; this cheerful decoration tended to be more delicate and feminine, and was prone to wear. Toward the end of the 1960s, do-it-yourself bag kits were introduced to coincide with the hippy-inspired craze for hobbies and crafts.

As well as box bags, Enid Collins produced canvas bags, decorated with similar designs, although these tend to attract less interest today. Many bags are signed "Enid Collins" or with a lower case "ec."

Wooden box bag by Enid Collins, with horse and carriage design, plastic handle, and leather strap fastening. Marked inside "Copyright 1966." ★★☆☆☆

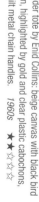

Shoulder tote by Enid Collins: beige canvas with black bird design, highlighted by gold and clear plastic cabochons, and gilt metal chain handles. *1960s* ★★☆☆☆

Handbag by Enid Collins: beige canvas with fruit and flower design, highlighted by gold and clear plastic cabochons.   *1960s*   ★ ★ ☆ ☆ ☆

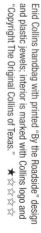

Enid Collins handbag with printed "By the Roadside" design and plastic jewels; interior is marked with Collins logo and "Copyright The Original Collins of Texas." ★ ☆☆☆☆

Enid Collins handbag with printed "Do-Drop In" design and plastic jewels.   ★ ☆ ☆ ☆

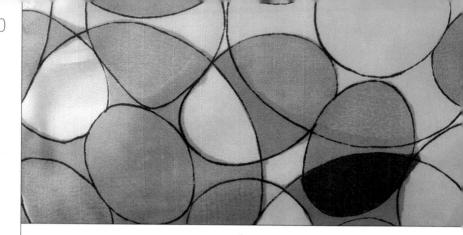

Bag by Ingber, USA. This bag is classic
1960s in style and design. ★☆☆☆☆

NOVELTY & PLASTIC

Vinyl bag with colored matchbook design and vinyl interior. *1960s* ★☆☆☆

Leopard-print felt bag by Ingber, USA, with gilt metal clasp and reinforced corners. *1950s–1960s* ★☆☆☆☆

American pink faux-snakeskin vinyl purse with silver plastic catch. Also has clear plastic internal purse stamped "Ethan Bags," on a gilt metal chain. *1960s* ★★☆☆☆

Translucent plastic handbag with gold vein decoration, by JR USA. *1950s* ★ ☆☆☆☆

White vinyl handbag with silk flower decoration covered by clear vinyl, and Perspex handle. ★ ☆☆☆☆

ANIMAL MAGIC

p.287

p.299

p.318

p.41

p.131

p.437

p.308

p.310

p.391

p.390

p.391

p.301

p.270

p.300

p.276

p.342

WALBORG
POODLE BAGS

Icons of 1950s glamor can sometimes appear rather kitsch, but this in no way decreases the demand for handbags with fun and frivolous motifs from the exuberant post-war period. As all eyes looked to France for fashion instruction, the French poodle became a symbol of chic sophistication in the US and Europe. Novelty poodle bags remain a particular favorite with collectors today.

American manufacturer Walborg is famed for its beaded bags and purses, and its shaped bags are extremely desirable. In the late 1940s, Walborg produced a line of black poodle purses hand-beaded in Belgium. It followed these in the 1950s with white poodles, hand-beaded in Japan. Both colors are the same size, equally rare, and of similar value. Walborg also made a black beaded cat purse. The cat, shown in a seated position, is exceptionally rare. Bags typically feature beaded "fur," and may have diamanté collars or gold-colored zippers.

American handbag by Jolles Original, with black velvet body, feather owl with glass bead eyes, bakelite and brass leaves, and Lucite handle. *1950s*

★★☆☆☆

Jolles Original bag, with applied beading, leaves, and plastic cherries; pink felt interior; white plastic handles; and gilt metal catch. ★★☆☆☆

Rare American wicker parasol purse, unmarked. *1950s* ★★★☆☆

Hand-made wooden "happy house" handbag. *1950s* ★ ★ ☆ ☆ ☆

Rare vanity case decorated with a print of the Fragonard painting *Girl on a Swing*. *1950s* ★★☆☆☆

"*All things feminine and beautiful with a touch of wit are what I love in a bag.*"

LULU GUINNESS, HANDBAG DESIGNER

Rigid handbag with velvet-covered exterior, brass frame, and plastic lid. *1950s* ★☆☆☆☆

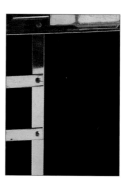

Jerry Terrence "Waste Basket: For Your Personal Trash" handbag, made from card and decorated with faux fur panel. ★ ☆ ☆ ☆

"Better a good plastic than a poor leather."

VOGUE MAGAZINE, C.1945

Orange plastic clutch bag, with metal frame, beige fabric lining, and gilt metal clasp. *1960s* ★☆☆☆☆

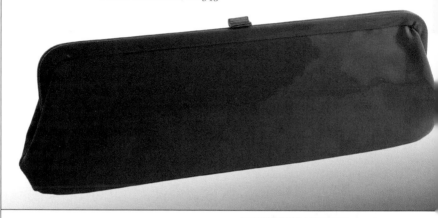

Red and black cylinder bag by Gaylene, with black change purse. *1960s* ★★☆☆☆

Sequined bag: made from craft kit, to be decorated by owner. Poodles are among the most popular designs and command higher prices. *Mid-to late 1960s* ★ ★ ☆ ☆ ☆

DETAIL: Fruit basket motifs on front.

THE CLASSIC 1950s BASKET

As handbags became more "boxy" in shape during the 1950s, designers revisited the humble straw shopping basket for inspiration. Baskets in all shapes, made from straw or raffia, were adorned with three-dimensional velvet flowers, real shells, or fabric berries, as well as other small objects such as faux pearls. The traditional woven basket had moved from a practical necessity to a decorative fashion item.

Although home-made in appearance, many examples were commercially produced and sold at popular holiday resorts such as Palm Springs. Novelty shapes, including animals and hats, are sought after today, as are hand-made Nantucket baskets, which are tightly woven and feature carved ivory plaques depicting seaside motifs. The wicker in all 1950s baskets tends to be delicate and liable to damage, as is the applied decoration. As a result, examples in good condition attract the most interest.

White woven basket with felt fruit decoration and gilt metal hardware. *1950s* ★☆☆☆☆

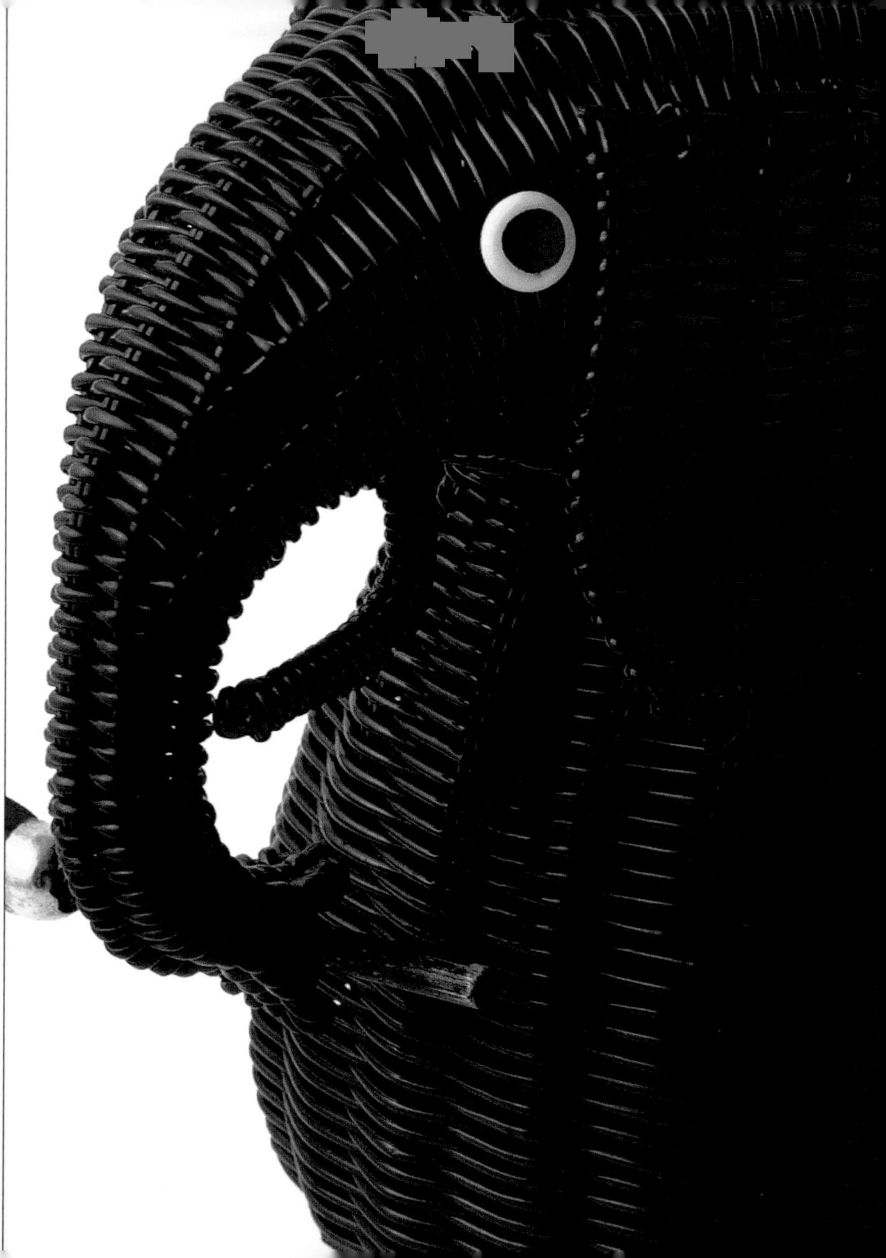

WICKER ANIMAL BAGS

Novelty bags are an expression of post-war frivolity. During the 1950s, fashions became less formal and so required less formal accessories. Add to this the buying power of the new teenage market, and the demand for novelty bags was assured.

Open baskets became a summer must-have. Manufacturers began to use wicker to create an amazing number of handbag creatures, including elephants, frogs, poodles, and fish. These animal shapes are particularly sought after by collectors today.

This wicker elephant is especially desirable because he comes with his own brush, which can be removed from his trunk and used to dust him down before a night out.

Rare American black wicker elephant purse with detachable brush; unmarked. *1950s* ★★★☆☆

Wicker shopping bag, with applied red felt panel and hand-sewn woolen poodles with rhinestone eyes. ★★☆☆☆

Chinese-made Mr Jonas wicker handbag, with cut-felt Scottie dogs covered by clear vinyl, and with label inside. *1950s* ★☆☆☆☆

Midas of Miami gold-painted straw and wicker handbag with black velvet panel, woven wool pcodle, sequins, and yellow-gold silk ining. *1950s* ★ ★ ☆ ☆ ☆

"You carry a bag as a badge of who you are."

LULU GUINNESS, HANDBAG DESIGNER

Unusual split oak basket bag, painted white with jeweled lid, by Jolles Original. ★ ☆ ☆ ☆ ☆

The front of this bag has a felt and fine bead decoration of flowers and leaves on a gold ground.

White wicker handbag, made in Hong Kong, with decorated front and gilt metal rope handle. *1950s–1960s* ★★☆☆

White wicker handbag, made in Hong Kong, with felt and fine bead mermaid, fish, and shell decoration, and white plastic handle. *1960s* ★★☆☆

Bag by Jolles Original, with applied poodle decoration. *1950s* ★ ☆☆☆☆

NOVELTY & PLASTIC

Unusual white wicker basket decorated with Lucite rosebuds and velvet ribbon leaves   *1950s*   ★ ☆☆☆☆

"It's all about proportion, shape, line, finish, fabric, balance."
TOM FORD, FORMER CREATIVE DIRECTOR, GUCCI

Volupté metal-case clutch bag with pink interior, retailed
by Bergdorf Goodman. *1950s*   ★ ☆☆☆☆

Judith Leiber bird minaudière, fitted with two small bird purses, hand-decorated with Swarovski crystals, and lined with gold kid leather. ★★★★★☆

JUDITH LEIBER

Born in Budapest in 1921, Judith Leiber trained as a handbag-maker before emigrating to New York, where she worked for a number of well-known companies, including Nettie Rosenstein. By 1963, Leiber had her own business, and in 1992 she won the Handbag Designer of the Year Award, followed two years later by a lifetime achievement award from The Council of Fashion Designers of America.

By far the most recognizable, and avidly collected, of her works are minaudières. Taken from the French word "to charm," these tiny bags were inspired by the small metal purses introduced by Van Cleef & Arpels in the 1930s. They are costly to produce as each bag is individually cast in metal and then covered with thousands of tiny Swarovski crystals, all applied by hand over a period of several days. Shapes include monkeys, cats, birds, and teddy bears. As well as minaudières, the Judith Leiber company still makes handbags in leather, suede, beadwork, and other luxurious materials.

DETAIL: The bird purses from inside the minaudière.

Judith Leiber-style penguin minaudière decorated with diamanté. ★★★★☆

> "I find that it is vital to have at least one type of handbag for each of the ten types of social occasion: Very Formal, Not so Formal, Just a Teensy Bit Formal, Informal But Not That Informal, Every Day, Every Other Day, Day Travel, Night Travel, Theater, and Fling."
>
> **MISS PIGGY**

DETAIL: Closed minaudière.

French hand-beaded evening purse with beaded frame and clasp and snake chain handle; unused. *1950s* ★★☆☆☆

French or Belgian bag with fine red glass beads, brass chain handle, and brass catch with rhinestone finial. *1950s* ★ ☆☆☆

DETAIL: Convertible bag with black cover.

Three-way convertible bag with detachable, reversible cover and gilt metal frame and handle. The cream and gold side is shown here. *1950s* ★☆☆☆☆

White beaded bag with colorful floral design; also has mother-of-pearl clasp and gilt metal chain strap. *1950s* ★★★☆☆

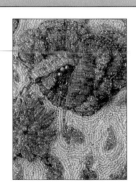

"Everybody has a 'model size' when it comes to handbags."

KARL LAGERFELD

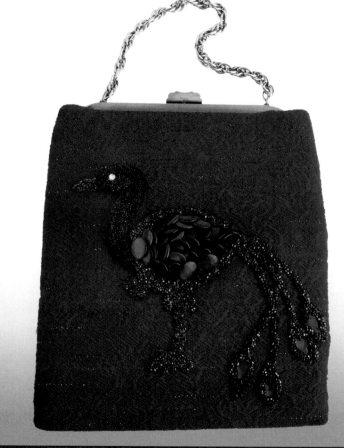

Red-beaded evening bag with black flamingo and gem detail, gilt metal clasp, and chain handle; in good condition. *1950s* ★★☆☆☆

BEADED & EMBROIDERED

☆☆☆
★★ ★

Black beaded and jeweled bag with poodle motif *1950s*

DETAIL: The manufacturer's mark inside the bag.

Guild Creations felt bag, with cathedral-style gilt metal frame set with paste stones. *1950s* ★ ☆ ☆ ☆ ☆

Hand-beaded evening purse with pastel flower design and beaded frame. Lining is labeled "Made in France, Saks, Fifth Avenue." *1950s* ★★☆☆☆

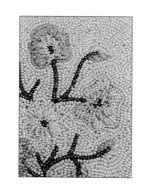

Black jersey jeweled and beaded tapestry handbag. *1950s* ★☆☆☆☆

Leather bag hand-decorated with flowers, leaves, and glass beads. *1950s* ★ ☆ ☆ ☆

The body of the bag is decorated with a floral design.

French evening purse, labeled "Made in France by Hand, Walborg." Frame has two Limoges porcelain plaques depicting an 18th-century courting couple. *1950s* ★ ★ ☆ ☆

Evening bag with faux pearls, small yellow and green glass beads, green bugle beads, and rhinestones; also has embossed metal frame and chain strap. Made in Hong Kong. *1950s* ★★☆☆☆

Belgian purse of white silk, with faceted iridescent glass and rope beads; also has gilt metal frame and clasp and cream silk lining. ★ ☆ ☆ ☆ ☆

Belgian purse with white and gold colored glass beads and ball clasp inset with faceted rhinestones. Cream silk lining is labeled "Jorelle Bags Made in Belgium." *1950s* ★☆☆☆☆

"*What do I think about the way most people dress? Most people are not something one thinks about.*"

DIANA VREELAND

Black beaded bag decorated with
gold flowers. *1950s* ★ ☆ ☆ ☆ ☆

French black satin handbag, custom-made, with double handles. ★ ★ ☆ ☆ ☆

Beaded and needlepoint-embroidered bag, marked "Made in Hong Kong," with beaded handle. *1950s* ★★★☆☆

Cream, pink, and blue beadwork purse, with gilt metal frame and chain handle, circular catch, and cream silk lining. *1950s* ★ ☆ ☆ ☆

French black evening bag with rhinestones, silver filigree frame, chain handle, and cream satin lining. *Early 1950s* ★★☆☆☆

Unsigned leather tote bag with needlework by Judith Leiber. This is an unusual Judith Leiber design. ★★★☆☆

Black bag with gold and black metal frame and leather handle. Decorated with painted banjo motif, plastic flowers, and faux gems. *1950s* ★★☆☆☆

Bag with picture entitled "La Maison du Poète." *1950s* ★★☆☆☆

Crocheted tote bag with applied strawberry decoration. ★ ☆ ☆ ☆

Tapestry bag with brown vinyl handle, gilt metal button clasp, and beige vinyl lining. *1960s* ★ ☆ ☆ ☆

Structured bag by Bobbie Jerome, New York: black velvet with circular brown Lucite handles and satin interior. *1960s* ★★☆☆☆

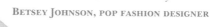

"Wow! Explode! The Sixties. It came to life in a pure, exaggerated, crazed out, wham, and wow way!"

BETSEY JOHNSON, POP FASHION DESIGNER

Handbag with matching clutch; both bags are unsigned. *1960s* ★☆☆☆☆

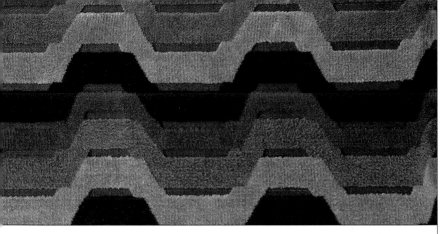

Sculpted chenille doctor's bag by Morris
Moskiwitz, signed "MM," with leather piping
and trim. *1960s–70s* ★★ ☆☆☆

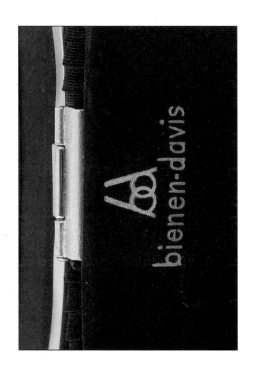

Bienen-Davis bags are made from high-quality materials, with stylish gilt metal frames. Often sculptural in shape, they epitomize an era when a neat appearance was de rigueur.

DETAIL: Maker's mark inside this box purse.

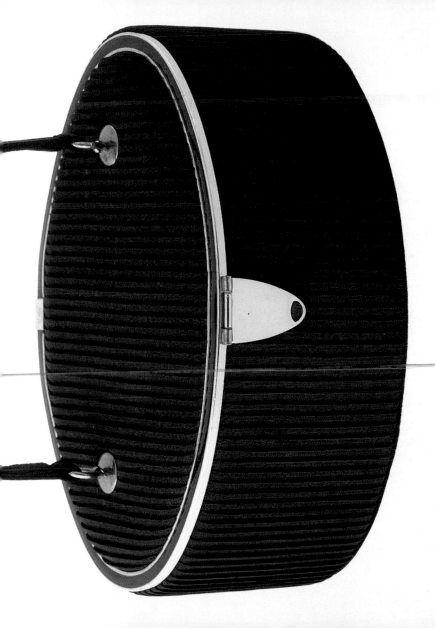

Enameled and pleated box purse by Bienen-Davis, the interior fitted with mirror and change purse. *1950s* ★ ☆☆☆☆

Wool purse with design depicting two donkeys eating daisies, and with faux tortoiseshell clasp, handle, and catch. Also has original purse and hand mirror. *1950s* ★★☆☆

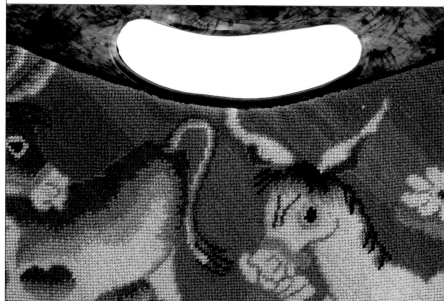

FABRIC

Rialto purse made from clear plastic over black fabric, with fruit and flower design. *1950s* ★ ☆ ☆ ☆

Carpet bag with gilt metal clasp and leather handles. *1960s* ★☆☆☆☆

Patchwork bag decorated with picture of musician. ★☆☆☆☆

Rare, reversible plaid bag with black trim and interior and vinyl glove holder strap; unsigned. *1950s* ★ ☆☆☆☆

Tapestry bag with Lucite handle and alternative cover, by L&M Edwards, UK. *1950s* ★ ☆☆☆☆

Hand Fashioned
Handbags

SOLD AROUND THE WORLD

by

Caron

DETAIL: Original Caron of Texas tag from inside bag.

FABRIC

★ ☆ ☆ ☆ ☆

Hand-decorated bag by Caron of Texas.   1950s

Fabric bag by Caron of Texas, hand-decorated with butterflies, jewels, and gold braid. ★☆☆☆☆

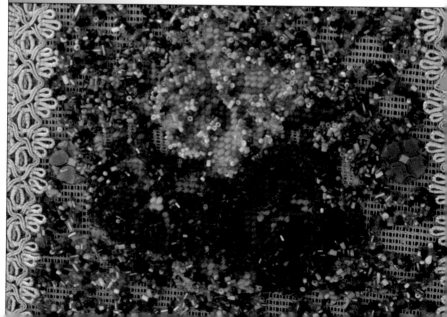

Tapestry bag by Caron of Texas, with applied leaves and sequins. ☆☆☆☆☆ ★

"A bag that's chic is a bag that you can wear everywhere, day or night. It has a sense of humor, a sort of tenderness."

SONIA RYKIEL, FASHION DESIGNER

Hand-decorated bag by Caron of Texas. *1950s* ★☆☆☆☆

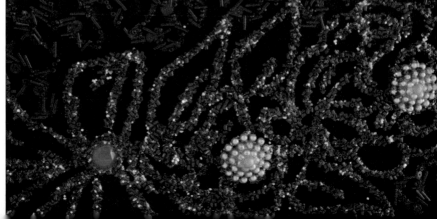

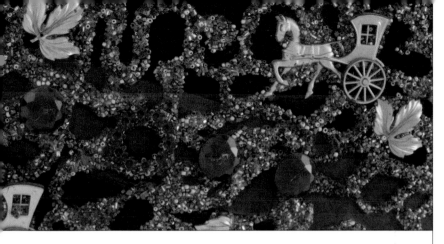

Fabric bag by Caron of Texas, hand-decorated with beads in a horse and carriage design. ★ ☆ ☆ ☆ ☆

Fabric bag by Caron of Texas, hand-decorated with butterflies and faux jewels. ★ ☆ ☆ ☆ ☆

Caron of Texas fabric bag, hand-decorated with flowers and gold braid. *1940s* ★ ☆ ☆ ☆

PUCCI

Vintage Pucci is unmistakable. The bold, geometric patterns and bright color schemes convey so much about the revolutionary design of the 1960s and 1970s. Emilio Pucci (1914–92) opened his first shop in 1949 in Capri, where he introduced "Capri Pants" and a huge range of exciting clothes and accessories in his signature prints. By the 1960s, he had established himself as a leading designer and was a key figure in the success of post-war Italian fashion design.

Pucci handbags, typically in vibrant psychedelic designs, are produced in high-quality materials such as silk and velvet, and are often finished with kid interiors and metal fastenings. The signature "Emilio" can often be found to the interior. In recent years the company has enjoyed a revival, with famous figures such as the pop star Madonna wearing Pucci creations.

Pucci handbag with waterfall front and gilt metal chain handle; in excellent condition. *1960s–70s* ★★★☆

DETAIL: Label inside Souré, New York, bag (opposite).

Black felt bag by Souré, New York, with diamanté and lace decoration, and gilt metal clasp. *1950s* ★ ☆ ☆ ☆ ☆

Black bag by Souré, New York, with brass frame and black plastic handle and body. Front is decorated with cornflowers made from white cloth, fine yellow beads, and amber cabochons.   *1950s*   ★★☆☆☆

FABRIC

Black fabric bag with floral embroidered panel and applied beads and leaves; probably by Souré, New York. *1950s* ★ ☆☆☆☆

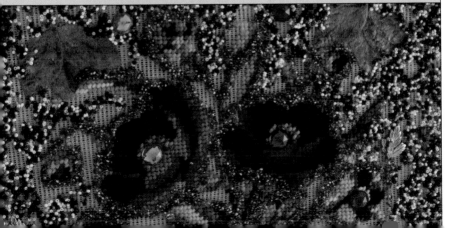

NOVEL IDEAS

p.102

p.346

p.292

p.243

p.291

p.344

p.290

p.187

p.185

p.187

p.436

p.414

p.376

p.439

NOVEL IDEAS

Plastic-coated linen bag by Souré, New York, with leather interior. Decorated with applied gold thread, studs, and porcelain plaques featuring pastoral vignettes. *1950s* ★ ☆☆☆☆

Black leather bag with figural tapestry panel, by Souré, New York. *1950s* ★ ★ ☆ ☆

Hand-decorated bag by Veldore of Texas, made from black fabric with floral motif and gold braid. *1950s* ★☆☆☆☆

Fabric bag by Veldore of Texas, decorated with hand-beaded country scene and gold braid. ★ ☆☆☆☆

Large tapestry and sculpted chenille bag by Nettie
Rosenstein, with satin lining. *1960s* ★★★☆☆

Tapestry bag by Nettie Rosenstein, with applied glass beads and satin lining; minor bead loss. *1950s* ★★☆☆

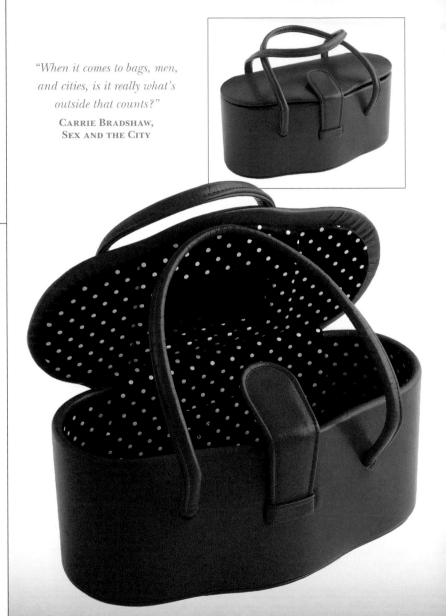

"When it comes to bags, men, and cities, is it really what's outside that counts?"

Carrie Bradshaw, Sex and the City

Red leather bucket bag, with two handles, polka-dot lining, and mirror inside lid. *Early 1950s* ★ ☆☆☆☆

Brown alligator-skin bag, stamped "Sydney California." *1950s* ★★☆☆☆

American black alligator-skin handbag, unmarked. *1950s* ★★☆☆☆

"The only real elegance is in the mind; if you've got that, the rest really comes from it."
DIANA VREELAND

DETAIL: Holzman mark inside bag.

ORIGINAL
by Holzman

LEATHER

Black calfskin bag by Holzman, USA, with Lucite clasp and circular handles. A rare, classic design. *1950s* ★★★☆☆

"It is the unseen, unforgettable,
ultimate accessory of fashion
that heralds your arrival and
prolongs your departure."
COCO CHANEL

American brown alligator-skin bag by Bellestone. *1950s* ★★☆☆☆

Purse by Holzman, USA, of leather with silkscreen print. Also has wrapped frame, piped edges, signature Holzman ball clasp, and silk lining. *Late 1950s–early 1960s* ★★☆☆☆

Black calfskin handbag by Holzman, USA, with Lucite handles and satin lining. *1950s* ★★☆☆☆

Alligator-skin bag with poodle clasps and red leather lining. Signed by Martin van Schaak, a New York-based designer who made unique bags for socialites. *1950s* ★★★☆☆

Lizardskin handbag with gilt metal hardware and clasp. *1950s* ★★☆☆☆

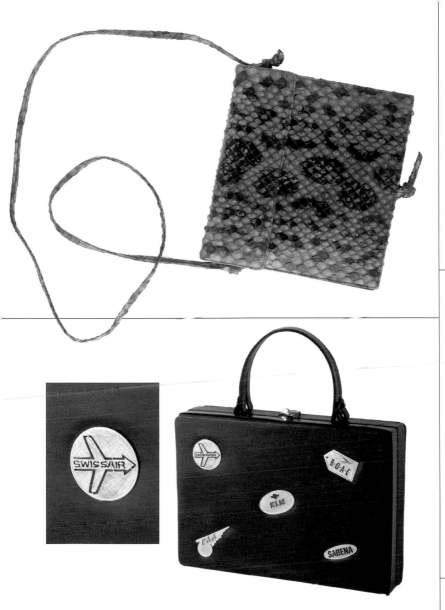

Green and black snakeskin shoulder bag, with three compartments and a tie at the bottom to draw them together. *1950s* ★★☆☆

Calfskin box purse by Murray Kruger, USA, with airline logos and signature blue leather fitted interior; retains matching change purse. *Late 1950s–early 1960s* ★★★☆

1950s–1960s

Vintage Gucci clutch bag: blue leather, with gilt metal interlocking "G" clasp. Stamped inside "Gucci of Italy." *Prob. 1950s* ★★☆☆☆

Gucci clutch bag: white patent leather, with gilt
metal interlocking "G" clasp. Stamped inside
"Gucci of Italy." *1960s* ★★☆☆☆

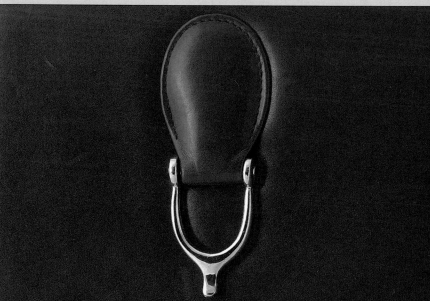

Gucci clutch bag of red calfskin, with shoulder strap and gilt metal catch. ★★☆☆☆

LEATHER

Gucci black lizardskin clutch bag, with gilt metal catch set with a blue stone cabochon. ★ ★ ☆ ☆

Black Gucci handbag with shoulder strap and gilt metal hardware. ★★★☆☆

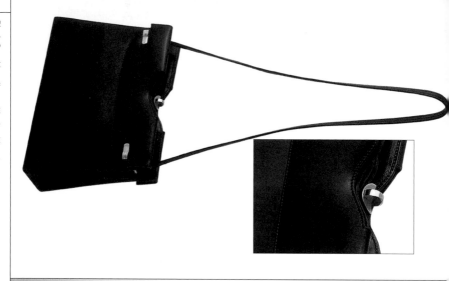

Dark brown crocodile-skin bag by Gucci, with gilt zmetal hardware and shoulder strap; in mint condition. ★★★★★

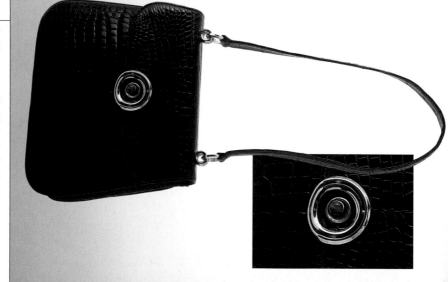

Gucci leather bag with woven effect finish, gilt metal clasp, and leather shoulder strap. *Early 1960s* ★ ☆ ☆ ☆ ☆

"A bag doesn't have to fit, and a bag
doesn't have to be comfortable."

LULU GUINNESS, HANDBAG DESIGNER

Black leather box bag, probably Italian, with
internal mirror and gilt metal reinforced
corners. *1960s* ★★☆☆☆

Yellow leather faux-crocodile handbag with gold-tone clasp. *1960s* ☆☆☆★ ★

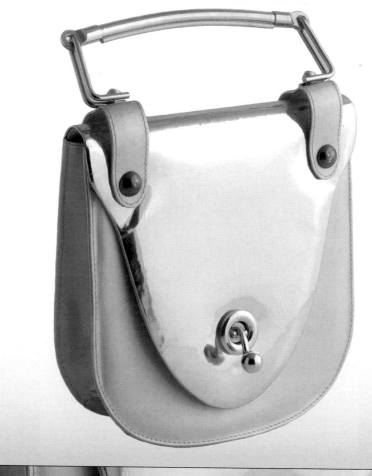

Patent white and gold leather handbag, with gold-tone metal handle and clasp. *1960s* ★★☆☆☆

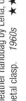

Red pebble leather handbag by Lena, USA, with gold-tone metal clasp. *1960s* ★ ★ ☆ ☆ ☆

Faux leopardskin bag by Ronay.   *1960s*   ★★☆☆☆

Faux cowhide satchel by Kadin, USA. *1960s* ★★☆☆☆

Rare faux ponyskin bag, unsigned but by Ronay. *1960s* ★★☆☆☆

DETAIL: Lining and signature inside bag.

Oblong clutch in patent leather by Ingber, with black and white striped lining. *1960s* ☆☆☆ ★★

Black calfskin leather handbag by De Leon, in elliptical design, with satin lining. This is a classic 1960s design. ★★☆☆☆

"*The loudest noise in our industry's recent history has been the whisper and tight snap of a handbag clasp.*"

HELEN STOREY, "FIGHTING FASHION," 1996

Spanish Coronado leather bag, with stitched detailing and brass clasp and feet. ★★★☆☆

Black leather handbag made in Italy for the O'Neil Company, with a gilt metal H-shaped clasp; similar in style to the Hermès Constance bag. ★☆☆☆☆

Ponyskin handbag with front pocket and gilt metal clasp and hardware. *1960s* ★ ★ ☆ ☆ ☆

Black crocodile-skin bag, with black enamel frame, marked "Genuine Crocodile." *1960s* ★ ★ ☆ ☆ ☆

DETAIL: Stamped mark inside Hermès bag, opposite.

HERMÈS

Stylish, unfussy bags by the house of Hermès have been delighting women since the 1880s, when Emile-Charles Hermès turned the attention of his Parisian leather-working company to producing wallets, cases, and handbags. Even in the early days, Hermès bags were known for their sturdy and functional shapes, which were updated in keeping with the fashions of the time. One of the greatest innovations was the introduction of a modern fastening: the recently invented "zipper."

Some of the classic Hermès designs have entered into fashion legend. The Kelly bag, launched in the 1950s and named after the film star Grace Kelly (who was famously photographed with one), was one of the most successful. Extremely sought after today, it can change hands for huge sums of money. Other bags that have caught public attention are the 1980s Birkin and the 1990s Macpherson bag.

Black box calfskin "Kelly" handbag by Hermès, with lock, keys and clochette. *1960s* ★★★★★

Rare turquoise alligator-skin box handbag by Nettie Rosenstein, with restored clasp and mirror. ★★★★★

Lizardskin box purse by Nettie Rosenstein, decorated with a gold wash. *1950s* ★ ★ ☆ ☆ ☆

Gold evening bag by Nettie Rosenstein, in vintage
condition with minor wear. *1960s* ★★☆☆☆

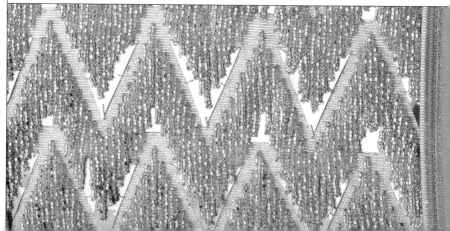

Brown crocodile-skin handbag by Nettie
Rosenstein. *1950s*. ★★★☆

DETAIL: Nettie Rosenstein's mark inside handbag.

NETTIE ROSENSTEIN

Austrian-born Nettie Rosenstein emigrated to the US as a child. She began her career as a milliner in 1927. By the 1930s she was working as a fashion designer, and began to make both handbags and costume jewelry to complement her clothes. Her handbags were made in the Italian city of Florence, a place renowned for its high-quality leather goods. Her couture designs were featured in *Vogue* magazine in the 1940s, and newspapers and magazines continued to publicize her designs throughout the 1950s and 1960s.

In 1961, Nettie Rosenstein stopped making clothes to concentrate on her accessory lines. Sometimes the influence of her costume jewelry line can be seen on the clasps of her handbags.

"Kelly"-style handbag by Nettie Rosenstein, with black flower design stamped on red leather and fabric-lined, fitted interior. *Late 1950s–early 1960s* ★ ★ ★ ☆ ☆

Nettie Rosenstein

*"Luxury must be comfortable,
otherwise it is not luxury."*

Coco Chanel

Black calfskin shoulder bag by Nettie Rosenstein, with glit fleur-de-lys design. *1960s* ★★☆☆

Black calfskin handbag by Nettie Rosenstein, with Art Nouveau-style gilt metal clasp.

★★★☆☆

Dark brown suede box purse by Nettie Rosenstein, with decorated clasp. *1950s–60s* ★★☆☆☆

Black box calfskin handbag by Nettie Rosenstein. *1950s* ★★★☆☆

Judith Leiber evening bag in black kurung snakeskin decorated with rhinestones. *Early 1960s* ★★★★☆

Judith Leiber black patent leather handbag with single handle and white metal clasp. *1960s* ★★☆☆

1970s– PRESENT

The best-known names of 20th-century handbag design were well established by the 1970s, but within a decade the trend for designer names had become an obsession. Names such as Chanel, Gucci, Fendi, and Hermès were must-haves on any stylish woman's arm. The obsession with such designer names continues to this day.

At the same time, the desire to stand out from the crowd with a novelty bag – first seen in the 1940s and 1950s – continued, with Dallas Handbags' telephone bags as well as other quirky forms, such as animals and magazine covers.

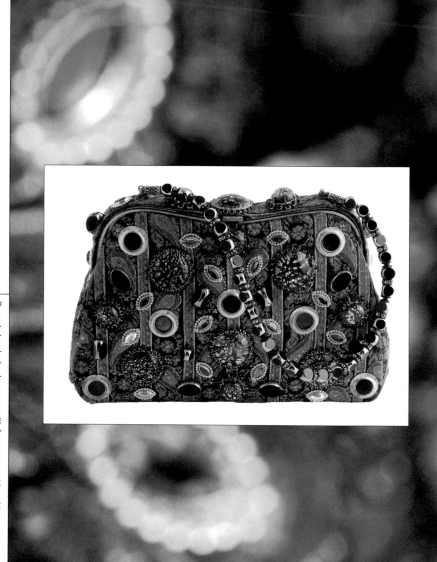

Brocade bag by La Jeunesse with faux gems set in gold metal, gold foil, and beaded chain strap set with multi-colored diamanté. *1970s* ★★★☆☆

DETAIL: Gilt metal maker's mark inside bag.

Velvet bucket bag with Lucite handle and brass button detail. *1970s* ★★☆☆☆

Floral suitcase-style handbag decorated with daisies. *1970s* ★ ☆☆☆

DETAIL: Cartoon refers to Coco Chanel's signature perfume, Chanel No. 5.

CHANEL

It's almost impossible to speak of 20th-century fashion without mentioning Coco Chanel (1883–1971). Her first shop opened in Paris in 1914, and by the 1920s she was one of the leading designers, producing everything from the little black dress to costume jewelry. The clean lines of her suits and the timeless style of her accessories earned her the devotion of women enjoying the new freedoms of the 1920s.

It was not until 1955 that she released her famous handbag, known as the "2.55." Chanel believed modern women should not be encumbered by a hand-held bag, so the 2.55 was designed to be like a French soldier's shoulder bag. It was diagonally hand-stitched to give it a quilted appearance. The house of Chanel still makes updated versions today.

Chanel enjoyed a revival from 1983, when Karl Lagerfeld took charge. He Introduced a wide variety of new designs, including the printed clutch bag shown here.

Chanel clutch bag: black patent leather with printed cartoon design of Coco Chanel. Also has original box.　2003　★★★☆☆

Clutch handbag by Chanel: cocoa-colored, pleated lambskin with lizardskin trim and retractable chain strap. *1970s* ★★★★☆

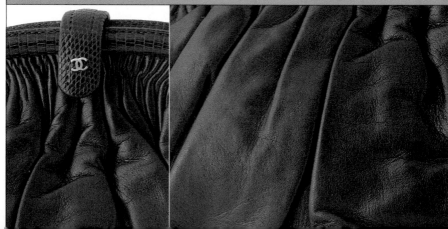

Purple leather Charles Jourdan shoulder bag with gilt metal frame and clasp. *1980s* ★★☆☆☆

Brown and black chenille shoulder bag by Carpet Bags of America. *1970s* ★☆☆☆☆

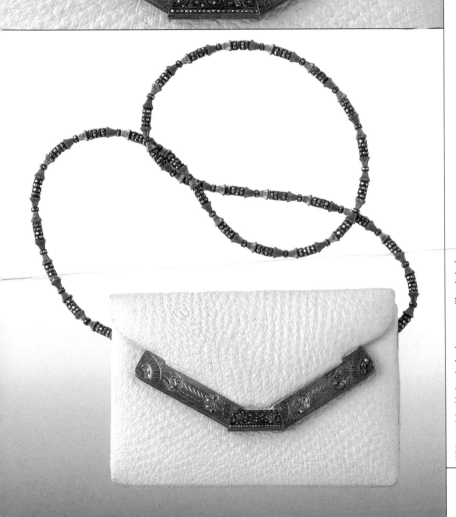

White ostrich-skin bag by La Jeunesse, with cut steel trim to front flap and shoulder strap. The bag is lined with gold leather. *Mid-1970s* ★ ★ ★ ☆ ☆

DETAIL: Stitched design and tortoiseshell closure.

FENDI

In the 1980s craze for glitz, glamor, and designer labels, fashion house Fendi was a runaway success. Newly power-suited women could enjoy their inflated pay checks by buying handbags with large price tags, such as those emblazoned with Fendi's "FF" logo.

The company first started to enjoy major acclaim, however, long before the 1980s. Fendi was established in Rome in 1925, as a small family leather and fur business, by Edoardo and Adele Fendi. By the end of the 1960s, it had become a respected name in Italian fashion, employing Karl Lagerfeld as designer. Its fur and leather goods were soon on sale in Bloomingdale's, New York.

In recent years, the "baguette" bag, introduced by the founder's granddaughter Silvia Venturini Fendi in 1997, has been hugely successful. Produced in a number of finishes and limited-edition variations, it has proved irresistible to many women — as has the spin-off, and much smaller, "croissant" bag.

Fendi brown leather purse with faux tortoiseshell closure and removabe leather strap; also has change purse. ★ ☆ ☆ ☆

"Envelope" clutch bag; fabric designed by Diane Love. *1980s* ★★☆☆☆

SPORTY

The 1980s saw an explosion in sports wear as street fashion. During the 1970s, female underwear had become less rigid and supportive, and the now ideal slim figure could only be achieved with rigorous exercise. At the same time, activities such as jogging and skateboarding came into fashion and sports stars became highly paid role models for young people worldwide. As a result, sports wear and accessories moved out of the gym and onto the catwalk.

People craved designer labels. This trend led heavily branded sports clothing manufacturers, such as Nike, Puma, and Adidas, to become global giants, producing a huge variety of bags. Other companies, such as Le Sportsac, concentrated solely on making bags, with outstanding results. Fashion designers, such as Ralph Lauren and Prada, were also influenced by the craze and introduced their own sporty bags.

Black crocodile-skin backpack, possibly by Ralph Lauren, with white metal clasp. *1980s* ★★☆☆☆

Paco Rabanne purple metal chain-mail shoulder bag; the metal plates are stamped with the designer's logo. *1980s–1990s* ★★★★★☆

Paco Rabanne black leather and silver aluminum disk bag; the disks are stamped with the designer's logo. *1980s* ★ ★ ★ ☆

Karung snakeskin and gilt metal box purse by Judith Leiber, fitted with mirror and tasseled comb and with original sleeper bag. *1970s* ★★☆☆☆

DETAIL: Signature plate on box purse.

Judith Leiber evening bag of brushed gold over metal, with coral accents and diamonds, clasp with coral top, and shoulder strap. *1970s* ★★★★☆

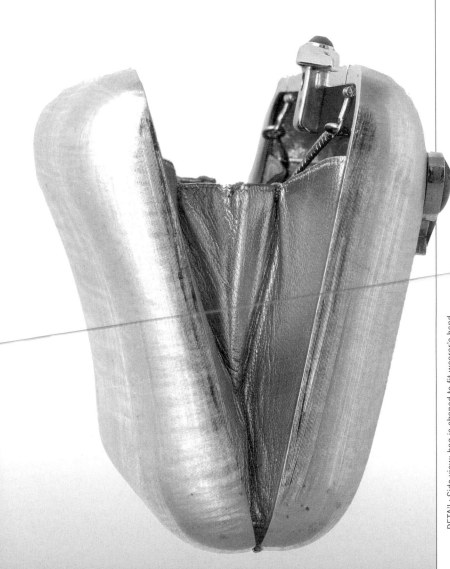

DETAIL: Side view; bag is shaped to fit wearer's hand.

American telephone bag by Dallas Handbags, in patent faux crocodile leather; in full working order. *1970s* ★★★★☆

These bags were the original mobile phone and a cult object in their day. They were designed to be plugged into a telephone socket and used to make calls.

Red plastic telephone bag by Dallas Handbags, with working telephone. *1970s* ★★☆☆☆

Merrythought novelty child's handbag, modeled as a soft toy rabbit. ★ ☆☆☆☆

DETAIL: Bag closure, showing strap and press stud.

MAGAZINE CLUTCH BAG

Modeled to resemble folded magazines, these bags are actually made from rigid plastic with a clear plastic sleeve encasing a replica magazine front cover. They are usually closed using a leather or plastic strap and press stud, and have a fabric lining. The clutch bags were manufactured in China and the US.

A great variety of magazine covers were used, from fashion titles (like the example shown on these pages) to travel guides. A chic fashion accessory in their day, magazine clutch bags are now a "must-have" among vintage handbags. The value of a bag depends on the condition of the plastic shell and the fastening, and on the condition and the subject of the paper insert.

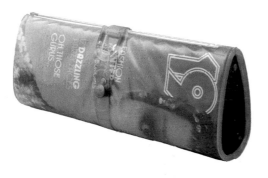

Clutch bag modeled as "19" magazine, with hard plastic body and clear plastic strap fastening. *1970s* ★ ☆ ☆ ☆ ☆

USING THE INTERNET

★ The internet has revolutionized the trading of collectibles as it provides a cost-effective way of buying and selling, away from the overheads of shops and auction rooms. Many millions of collectibles are offered for sale and traded daily, with sites varying from global online marketplaces, such as eBay, to specialist dealers' websites.

★ When searching online, remember that some people may not know how to accurately describe their item. General category searches, even though more time consuming, and even purposefully misspelling a name, can yield results. Also, if something looks too good to be true, it probably is. Using this book to get to know your market visually, so that you can tell the difference between a real bargain and something that sounds like one, is a good start.

★ As you will understand from buying this book, color photography is vital – look for online listings that include as many images as possible and check them carefully. Beware that colors can appear differently, even between computer screens.

★ Always ask the vendor questions about the object, particularly regarding condition. If there is no image, or you want to see another aspect of the object – ask. Most sellers (private or trade) will want to realize the best price for their items so will be more than happy to help – if approached politely and sensibly.

★ As well as the "e-hammer" price, you will probably have to pay additional transactional fees such as packing, shipping, and possibly regional or national taxes. It is always best to ask for an estimate of these additional costs before leaving a bid. This will also help you tailor your bid as you will have an idea of the maximum price the item will cost if you are successful.

★ As well as the well-known online auction sites, such as eBay, there is a host of other online resources for buying and selling, for example fair and auction date listings.

MUSEUMS

Australia

Katoomba Purse Museum
Katoomba, Australia
info@pursemuseum.com.au

Canada

Textile Museum of Canada
55 Centre Avenue
Toronto, Ontario
M5G 2H5, Canada
info@textilemuseum.ca
www.textilemuseum.ca

Royal Ontario Museum
100 Queen's Park
Toronto, Ontario M5S 2C6, Canada
www.rom.on.ca

France

Musée de la Mode et du Textile
107, rue de Rivoli
75001 Paris
www.ucad.fr

Germany

Deutsches Ledermuseum
Frankfurter Straße 86
63067 Offenbach
info@ledermuseum.de
www.ledermuseum.de

Holland

Tassenmuseum HENDRIKJE
(Museum of Bags and Purses)
Zonnestein 1, 1181 LR Amstelveen
www.tassenmuseum.nl

UK

Fashion and Textile Museum
83 Bermondsey St.
London SE1 3XF
Email: info@ftmlondon.org

The Victoria and Albert Museum
South Kensington
Cromwell Road
London SW7 2RL
www.vam.ac.uk

Museum of Costume
Bennett Street
Bath BA1 2QH
www.museumofcostume.co.uk

Museum of London
London Wall
London EC2Y 5HN
www.museumoflondon.org.uk

Fashion and Textile Museum
83 Bermondsey St.
London SE1 3XF
Email: info@ftmlondon.org

USA

The Textile Museum
2320 S Street, NW
Washington, DC 20008-4088
www.textilemuseum.org

Phoenix Art Museum
McDowell Road & Central Avenue
1625 N. Central Avenue
Phoenix, AZ 85004
www.phxart.org

Smithsonian Institution
The National Mall
NW Washington DC
www.si.edu

Metropolitan Museum of Art
1000 5th Avenue
New York
NY 10028-0198 USA
www.metmuse

Phoenix Art Museum
Central Avenue & McDowell Road
1625 N. Central Ave.
Phoenix, AZ 85004-1685
www.phxart.org

**The Museum at the Fashion
Institute of Technology**
Seventh Avenue at 27 Street
New York City 10001-5992
www.fitnyc.edu

**Museum of Fine Arts,
Boston Avenue of the Arts**
465 Huntington Ave.
Boston, MA 02115-5523
www.mfa.org

The Philadelphia Museum of Art
26th Street and the
Benjamin Franklin
Parkway
Philadelphia, PA 19130
www.philamuseum.org

DEALERS AND AUCTION HOUSES

Sanford Alderfer Auction Company
501 Fairgrounds Rd,
Hatfield, PA 19440, USA
Tel: 001 215 393 3000
www.alderferauction.com

Andrea Hall Levy
PO Box 1243,
Riverdale, NY 10471, USA
Tel: 001 646 441 1726
barangrill@aol.com

Antique Textiles and Lighting
Antique Textiles,
34 Belvedere,
Landsdowne Road,
Bath, BA1 5HR
Tel: 01225 310 795
www.antiquetextilesandlighting.co.uk

Bucks County Antique Center
Route 202, PA 18914, USA
Tel: 001 215 794 9180

Beyond Retro
110–112 Cheshire St.,
London E2 6EJ
Tel: 020 7613 3636
Tel: 020 7613 3636
sales@beyondretro.com
www.beyondretro.com

Bonny Yankauer
bonnyy@aol.com

Cloud Cuckoo Land
6 Charlton Place,
Camden Passage,
London N1 8EA
Tel: 020 7354 3141

Cheffins
Clifton House
1&2 Clifton Road,
Cambridge,
Cambridgeshire CB1 7EA
Tel: 01223 213 343
www.cheffins.co.uk

Cristobal
26 Church Street,
London NW8 8EP
Tel/Fax: 020 7724 7230
www.cristobal.co.uk

Decodame.com
853 Vanderbilt Beach Road,
PMB 8, Naples,
FL 34108, USA
Tel: 001 239 514 6797
www.decodame.com

Deco Jewels Inc.
131 Thompson Street,
NY, USA
Tel: 001 212 253 1222
decojewels@earthlink.net

David Rago Auctions
333 North Main Street,
Lambertville,
NJ 08530, USA
Tel: 001 609 397 9374
www.ragoarts.com

Design20c
www.design20c.com

Fellows & Sons
Augusta House,
19 Augusta St,
Hockley,
Birmingham B18 6JA
Tel: 0121 212 2131
Fax: 0121 212 1249
info@fellows.co.uk
www.fellows.co.uk

Fantiques
Tel: 020 8840 4761
paula.raven@ntlworld.com

Fayne Landes Antiques
593 Hansell Road,
Wynnewood, PA 19096 USA
Tel: 001 610 658 0566

Freeman's
1808 Chestnut Street,
Philadelphia, PA 19103,
USA
Tel: 001 215 563 9275
www.freemansauction.com

Nancy Goldsmith
New York
Tel: 001 212 696 0831

John Jesse
160 Kensington Church St.,
London W8 4BN
Tel: 020 7229 0312
jj@johnjesse.com

Linda Bee
Grays Antique Market Mews,
1-7 Davies Street,
London W1Y 2LP
Tel: 020 7629 5921
www.graysantiques.com

Manic Attic
Stand S011,
Alfies Antiques Market,
13 Church St,
London NW8 8DT
Tel: 020 7723 6105
Fax: 020 7724 0999
manicattic@alfies.clara.net

Marc Menzoyan
Cité des Antiquaires,
117 boulevard Stalingrad,
69100 Lyon-Villeurbane,
France
Tel.: 00 33 (0)4 78 81 50 81

Mendes Antique Lace and Textiles
Tel: 01273 203 317
www.mendes.co.uk

Mix Gallery
17 South Main Street,
Lambertville, NJ 08530,
USA
Tel: 001 609 773 0777
www.mix-gallery.com

Moderne Gallery
111 North 3rd Street,
Philadelphia, PA 19106,
USA
Tel: 001 215 923 8536
www.modernegallery.com

**The Multicoloured
Time Slip**
Unit S002,
Alfies Antiques Market,
13-25 Church St,
London NW8 8DT
Mob: 07971 410 563
d_a_cameron@hotmail.
com

Neet-O-Rama
93 West Main St,
Somerville,
NJ 08876 USA
Tel: 001 908 722 4800
www.neetstuff.com

**Otford Antiques and
Collectors Centre**
26-28 High St,
Otford, Kent TN14 5PQ
Tel: 01959 522 025
www.otfordantiques.co.uk

Pook and Pook
463 East Lancaster Ave,
Downington, PA 19335,
USA
Tel: 001 610 269
4040/0695 www.
pookandpook.com

Quittenbaum
Kunstauktionen München
Hohenstaufenstraße 1,
D-80801,
Munich, Germany
Tel: 00 49 89 33 00 75 6
www.quittenbaum.de

Axtell Antiques
1 River St.,
Deposit, NY 13754 USA
Tel: 001 607 467 2353
www.axtellantiques.com

Richard Gibbon
34/34a Islington Green,
London N1 8DU
Tel: 020 7354 2852
neljeweluk@aol.com

Ritzy
7 The Mall Antiques Arcade,
359 Upper Street,
London N1 0PD
Tel: 020 7704 0127

Roxanne Stuart
PA, USA
gemfairy@aol.com

Red Roses
Vintage Modes,
Grays Antique Market,
1–7 Davies Mews,
London W1Y 2PL
Tel: 020 7409 0400
sallie_ead@lycos.com
www.vintagemodes.co.uk

Steinberg and Tolkien
193 King's Road,
Chelsea, London SW3 5ED
Tel: 020 7376 3660

Sheila Cook
283 Westbourne Grove,
London, W11 2QA
Tel: 020 7792 8001
www.sheilacook.co.uk

Sara Covelli
Private Collection

**Sparkle Moore at The Girl
Can't Help It**
G100 & G116,
Alfies Antique Market,
13 Church St,
London NW8 8DT
Tel: 020 7724 8984
sparkle.moore@virgin.net
www.sparklemoore.com

The Design Gallery
5 The Green,
Westerham, Kent TN16 1AS
Tel: 01959 561 234
www.designgallery.co.uk

Pam Ferrazuti
Toronto Antiques Centre,
276 King Street West,
Toronto, Ontario, M5V 1J2
Canada
Tel: 001 416 260 0325
http://www.
pamferrazuttiantiques.com

**Kunst-Auktionshaus
Martin Wendl**
August-Bebel-Straße 4,
07407 Rudolstadt, Germany
Tel: 00 49 3672 4243 50
Tel: 00 49 3672 4243 50

Woolley & Wallis
51–61 Castle St,
Salisbury, Wilts. SP1 3SU
Tel: 01722 424 500
Fax: 01722 424 508
enquiries@woolleyand
wallis.co.uk
www.woolleyandwallis.
co.uk

INDEX

PICTURE CREDITS

The following images, photographed with permission from the sources itemized below are copyright © Judith Miller and Dorling Kindersley.

Andrea Hall Levy p.56, p.66, p.67, p.68, p.75, p.76, p.94, p.95, p.109, p.110, p.131, p.139, p.148, p.149, p.152, p.155, p.161, p.166, p.169, p.171, p.175, p.177, p.188, p.196, p.202, p.207, p.208, p.210, p.212, p.218, p.227, p.290, p.316, p.317, p.318, p.324, p.330, p.332, p.370, p.378, p.396, p.397, p.414, p.416, p.436; **Antique Textiles and Lighting** p.12, p.13, p.18, p.27, p.28, p.69, p.73, p.80, p.83, p.86, p.93 **Axtell Antiques** p.30, p.31; **Beyond Retro** p.347; **Bonny Yankauer** p.46, p.62, p.93, p.130, p.132, p.143, p.325; **Bucks County Antique Center** p.29; **Cheffins** p.104, p.105 **Cloud Cuckoo Land** p.304; **Cristobal** p.126, p.141, p.145, p.151, p.160, p.161, p.164, p.174, p.183, p.187, p.189, p.190, p.219, p.220, p.221, p.235, p.251, p.288, p.303, p.313, p.360;

Deco Dame p.98, p.101, p.112; **Deco Jewels Inc.** p.220, p.223, p.224, p225, p.228, p.237, p. 232, p.238, p.239, p.241, p.242, p.243, p.245, p.246, p.247, p.248, p.250, p.253, p.254, p.255, p.256, p.257, p.258, p.259, p.260, p.262, p.263, p.264, p.265, p.436; **David Rago Auctions** p.332, p.425; **Design20c** p.439; **The Design Gallery** p.64, p.77, p.136, p.194, p.205, p.209; **Fellows & Sons** p.437; **Fantiques** p.144, p.146, p.173, p.174, p.229, p.282, p.283, p.289, p.295, p.302, p.305, p.306, p.314, p.315, p. 321, p.323, p.328, p.349, p.350, p.351, p.352, p.353, p. 354, p.355, p.359, p.361, p.364, p.366, p.367; **Fayne Landes Antiques** p.43, p.45, p.48, p.54; **John Jesse** p.102; **Kunst-Auktionshaus** p.58; **Nancy Goldsmith** p.211, p.273, p.329, p.379, p.423, p.426, p.434;

Linda Bee p.276, p.277, p.386, p.387, p.388, p.422, p.429; **Manic Attic** p.283, p.300; **Marc Menzoyan** p.347, p.396; **Mendes Lace and Textiles** p.10, p.37, p.87, p.91; **Mix Gallery** p.197, p.201, p.203, p.280, p.294, p.333, p.337, p. 338, p.339, p.341, p.346, p.357, p.368, p.369, p.373, p.376, p.377, p.378, p.379, p.389, p. 390, p.391, p.393, p.394, p. 399, p.400, p.401, p. 402, p.403, p.405, p.407, p.408, p.409, p.410, p.411, p.420, p.422, p.430, p.431, p.432; **Moderne Gallery** p.182; **The Multicoloured Time Slip** p.421; **Neet-O-Rama** p.269, p.270, p.278, p.279, p.281, p.343, p.417; **Otford Antiques and Collectors Centre** p.168; **Pam Ferrazuti** p.82; **Pook and Pook** p.15, p.19; **Private Collection** p.127, p.142, p.191, p.198, p.199, 418; **Quittenbaum** p.111;

Richard Gibbon p.116, p.153, p.154, p.186, p.204, p.208, p.213, 290, p.298, p.312, p.317, p.322, p.323, p.371, p.375, p.397; **Ritzy** p.175; **Roxanne Stuart** p41, p.81, p.89, p.92, p.137, p.147, p.158, p.164, p.165, p.193, p.195, p.233, p.234, p.235, p.282, p.294, p.300, p.326, p.331, p.342, p.345; **Sanford Alderfer Auction Company** p.36, p.44, p.52, p.53, p.58, p.59, p.60, p.61, p.90, p.99, p. 113, p.170, p.180, p.292; **Sara Covelli** p.49, p.72, p.103; **Steinberg and Tolkien** p.11, p.23, p.25, p.42, p.145, p.157, p.159, p.181, p.229, p.271, p.292, p.308, p.310, p.344; **Sheila Cook** p176, p.180, p.275; **Sparkle Moore at The Girl Can't Help It** p.251, p.268, p.272, p.291, p.293, p.297, p.299, p.301, p.319, p.322, p.365; **Woolley & Wallis** p.106

ARCHIVE PICTURE ACKNOWLEDGMENTS

The publisher would like to thank the following for their kind permission to reproduce their material.

pp.8–9: **Mary Evans Picture Library**; pp.34–35: **Mary Evans Picture Library**; pp.114–115: **Corbis/ Condé Nast Archive**; pp.214–215: **Corbis/ Condé Nast Archive**; pp.412–413: **Camera Press/Marie Claire/ Antone/Nathalie Suret**.

All other images © Dorling Kindersley and The Price Guide Company Ltd.
For further information see: www.dkimages.com

All jacket images © Dorling Kindersley and The Price Guide Company Ltd.

ACKNOWLEDGMENTS

AUTHOR'S ACKNOWLEDGMENTS

The Price Guide Company would like to thank the following for their contribution to the production of this book:

Photographer Graham Rae for his wonderful photography.

All of the dealers, auction houses, and private collectors for kindly allowing us to photograph their collections, especially Linda Bee, Janice Berkson, Richard Gibbon, Andrea Hall Levy, Cheri Lynne, Stephen Miners, Chrissie Painell, Paula Raven, Roxanne Stuart, Yai Thammachote, and Bonny Yankauer.

Also special thanks to Jessica Bishop, Dan Dunlavey, Mark Hill, Sandra Lange, Cathy Marriott, Claire Smith, and Sara Sturgess for their editorial contribution and help with image sourcing.

Thanks also to Digital Image Co-ordinator Ellen Sinclair and Workflow Consultant Bob Bousfield.

PUBLISHER'S ACKNOWLEDGMENTS

Dorling Kindersley would like to thank the following for their contribution to the production of this book:

Sarah Smithies for picture research, Sara Sha'ath for proofreading, Tamsin Curtis for proofreading and co-ordinating proofs, Dawn Henderson and Kathryn Wilkinson for additional editorial help, and Dorothy Frame for indexing.